# QUIZ BOOK for cleVer Kids

Compiled and edited by
Lauren Farnsworth
Illustrations by Chris Dickason

Designed by Jack Clucas
Cover design by Angie Allison

Special thanks to Nicola Baxter

# QUIZ BOOK
# for clever Kids

Buster Books

First published in Great Britain in 2015 by Buster Books,
an imprint of Michael O'Mara Books Limited,
9 Lion Yard, Tremadoc Road, London SW4 7NQ

 www.mombooks.com/buster

Buster Books

@BusterBooks

A CIP catalogue record for this book is available from the British Library.

ISBN: 978-1-78055-314-6

8  10  9

Papers used by Buster Books are natural, recyclable products
made from wood grown in sustainable forests. The manufacturing processes
conform to the environmental regulations of the country of origin.

Printed and bound in September 2019 by CPI Group (UK) Ltd,
108 Beddington Lane, Croydon, CR0 4YY, United Kingdom

MIX
Paper from
responsible sources
FSC® C020471

# INTRODUCTION

Are you ready for a challenge? This book contains over 600 quizzical questions which are designed to test even the cleverest kid. There are ten different kinds of quiz to keep you on your toes. Each set of questions can be tackled on its own, but the quizzes are divided into sections and get steadily harder as the book progresses.

At the end of every section, there is a space for you to write down how many questions you got right. You can work out your scores by checking the answers at the back of the book.

Read the simple instructions on each page before tackling a quiz. It might also be a good idea to work in pencil so you can rub out answers if you change your mind. If you get stuck on a question, why not scribble down a guess?

You could also try asking an adult for answers, but did you know that your brain is actually much more powerful than a grown-up's? When people get older, their brains get rid of lots of bits of information they think they don't need, which means you might be better at solving these quizzes than older people are.

Let the quizzing begin. Good luck and have fun!

LEVEL
ONE

## QUIZ SHOW: POLAR REGIONS

These questions are simple multiple choice. The correct answer will always be either a, b or c. But which one?

1. **What is the area around the North Pole called?**
   a. The Antarctic
   b. The Arctic
   c. Alaska

2. **Why does a compass needle point North?**
   a. Because of the way it is shaped
   b. The Earth is like a magnet and the needle points to the Earth's magnetic North Pole
   c. There are more magnetic particles at the North Pole than anywhere else on the planet

3. **Both the Arctic and Antarctic are famous for being very, very cold. Which one is colder?**
   a. The Antarctic
   b. Both are about the same
   c. The Arctic

4. **Are the North and South Pole on water or on land?**
   a. The South Pole is on water, the North Pole is on land
   b. They are both on land
   c. The North Pole is on water, the South Pole is on land

5. **The polar regions are cold, but are they also wet?**
   a. It doesn't rain often, but regularly
   b. No, they are mainly as dry as a desert
   c. Yes, several metres (yards) of snow fall every year

6. **What time zone is the South Pole in?**
   a. Greenwich Mean Time (UK)
   b. None, because many time zones meet there
   c. Eastern Time Zone (New York)

7. **How long does a 'polar' day last from sunrise to sunset?**
   a. Several weeks
   b. Six months
   c. One day

# MISSING WORDS: ANIMALS

The sentences below each have a word missing. Pick the correct word from the box next to each sentence and write it in the space.

**1.** Fetlock, withers, hock and mane are parts of a

_____.

Lion
Horse
Beetle

Deer
Hare
Dog

**2.** The young of a _____ is called a fawn.

**3.** A queen bee, a worker bee and a _____ bee are the three types of bee in a bee colony.

Drone
Marcher
Stinger

Horse
Duck
Camel

**4.** Bactrian and dromedary are types of _____.

**5.** A spider has _____ legs.

Four
Eight
Ten

Fox
Cat
Horse

**6.** A vixen is a female

_____ .

**7.** Polar bears live in the Arctic

and penguins live in the

_____ .

Antarctic
Archatic
Accatic

Rabbit
Badger
Butterfly

**8.** A _____ lives in a sett.

# TRUE OR FALSE: INSECTS

Are the statements below true or false? Tick the box you think is correct.

### 1. Insects 'breathe' through little holes called spiracles.

☐ 👍 True or false? 👎 ☐

### 2. A bee uses its teeth to sting.

☐ 👍 True or false? 👎 ☐

### 3. Malaria is spread by mosquitoes.

☐ 👍 True or false? 👎 ☐

### 4. Some honey bees live in a hive.

☐ 👍 True or false? 👎 ☐

### 5. Worms are kept in a vespiary.

☐ 👍 True or false? 👎 ☐

### 6. All bees make honey.

☐ 👍 True or false? 👎 ☐

### 7. Insects make up approximately 80 per cent of the total number of animal species on Earth.

☐ 👍 True or false? 👎 ☐

8. A python is a poisonous flying beetle.

☐ 👍 True or false? 👎 ☐

9. A weevil is a type of butterfly.

☐ 👍 True or false? 👎 ☐

10. The three sections of an insect's body are called the head, thorax and abdomen.

☐ 👍 True or false? 👎 ☐

11. Insects have skeletons inside their bodies.

☐ 👍 True or false? 👎 ☐

12. All insects have wings.

☐ 👍 True or false? 👎 ☐

13. Insects have hearts identical in structure to humans'.

☐ 👍 True or false? 👎 ☐

14. A baby insect is often called a larva.

☐ 👍 True or false? 👎 ☐

15. Ants live in a colony.

☐ 👍 True or false? 👎 ☐

# OUT OF ORDER: ANIMALS

The words in the lists below are all in the wrong order. Read the instructions above each list and then place the words in the correct order by rewriting them in the spaces on the right.

## 1. Place these animals by size, largest first.

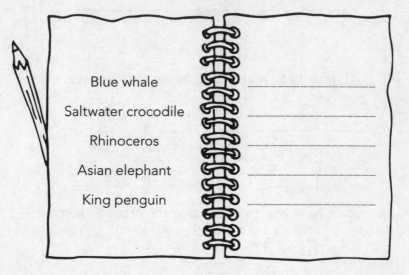

Blue whale

Saltwater crocodile

Rhinoceros

Asian elephant

King penguin

### 2. Place these animals by speed, fastest first.

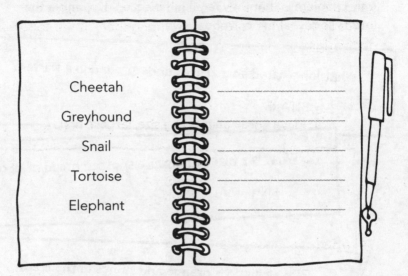

Cheetah

Greyhound

Snail

Tortoise

Elephant

### 3. Place these birds by size, largest first.

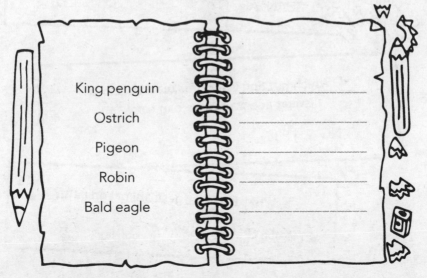

King penguin

Ostrich

Pigeon

Robin

Bald eagle

# WORD JUMBLE: ANIMALS

The answers are given to all these questions below. The only problem is that they're all jumbled up. Unjumble the letters to reveal the correct answer.

1. What long-eared animal lives underground in a warren?

BITARB _____

2. What is a black and white spotted breed of dog?

ANITAMADL _____

3. Which ape is orange and swings in the trees?

GUANTARON _____

4. Which buzzing insect makes a delicious sweet substance we can eat?

NOYEH EBE _____

5. What is the largest animal on land?

CFRAINA PLENTEHA _____

# Quiz 5

Score.........................................

**6. Which large land animal likes to wallow in mud?**

MOTAPIPOHUSP

_____

**7. Which bird carries fish in its sack-like bill?**

NILEPCA

_____

**8. Which animal lives in a group called a pride?**

ONLI

_____

**9. Which type of animal became extinct many millions of years ago?**

ISONDARU

_____

**10. What do we call an animal that lives on dry land and in water?**

PHIMABANI

_____

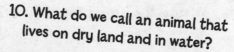

# HALL OF FAME: ANIMALS

The multiple-choice questions below are all things that deserve a place in a hall of fame. Test your knowledge on the world's biggest, brightest and best.

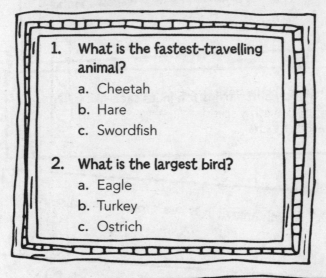

1. **What is the fastest-travelling animal?**
   a. Cheetah
   b. Hare
   c. Swordfish

2. **What is the largest bird?**
   a. Eagle
   b. Turkey
   c. Ostrich

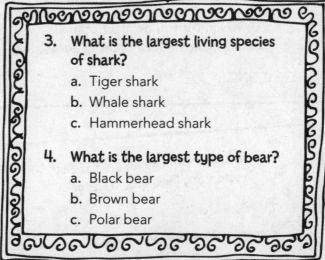

3. **What is the largest living species of shark?**
   a. Tiger shark
   b. Whale shark
   c. Hammerhead shark

4. **What is the largest type of bear?**
   a. Black bear
   b. Brown bear
   c. Polar bear

## Quiz 6

**5. What is the largest beetle?**
   a. Goliath beetle
   b. Ladybird
   c. Stag beetle

**6. What is the largest spider?**
   a. Black widow spider
   b. Funnel spider
   c. Goliath birdeater tarantula

**7. What is the fastest travelling fish?**
   a. Whale shark
   b. Sailfish
   c. Barracuda

**8. What is the largest lizard?**
   a. Chameleon
   b. Komodo dragon
   c. Gecko

**9. What is the slowest-moving land animal?**
   a. Three-toed sloth
   b. Garden snail
   c. Tortoise

**10. What is the world's most popular pet?**
   a. Dog
   b. Cat
   c. Bird

## MATCH UP: COLOURS

Below are three sets of lists. Each word in the left-hand list can be matched up with a word in the right. Match all the words until they are all paired up.

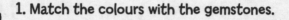

### 1. Match the colours with the gemstones.

| | |
|---|---|
| Red o | o Diamond |
| Green o | o Ruby |
| Blue o | o Sapphire |
| White o | o Emerald |
| Purple o | o Amber |
| Orange o | o Amethyst |

## 2. Match the colours with the fruits.

Purple o                    o Strawberry

Red o                       o Blueberry

Yellow o                    o Grapes

Blue o                      o Banana

Orange o                    o Satsuma

## 3. Match up these colours with the flowers.

Yellow o                    o Cherry blossom

Red o                       o Sunflower

Purple o                    o Violet

Pink o                      o Poppy

Blue o                      o Cornflower

## GUESS WHAT: ANIMALS

The sentences below all describe certain animals. Try to guess what the answer is from the descriptions.

1.  I have long legs and a long neck so I can reach the leaves in the trees. I have a blue tongue.

2.  I move very slowly and spend most of my life asleep. I like to hang in the trees away from predators.

3.  I am a tropical, colourful bird that is well-known for being taught to speak.

4.  I live in Australia and I like to jump around. I am a large animal and can be fierce.

5.  I am very small but I can carry up to 100 times my own body weight. I like living in a big colony.

6.  I live on the African plains and am famous for the noises I make that sound like laughter.

7.  I like to be awake at night so I can hunt for mice. I have big, round eyes and sharp talons.

**8.** I am very long and have no legs. I have to lie in the sun before I can move. Sometimes I have fangs that inject poison.

**9.** I live in the countryside and cities. I have a sleek red coat and my woodland home is called a den.

**10.** I am a bird who likes to sit in trees and peck at the bark very fast.

**11.** I am the biggest animal on the planet and I live in the ocean.

**12.** I am a common household pet. I come in many different breeds, and might like to play games such as fetching a stick.

**13.** I am a large cat found mainly in Africa, with a terrific roar. If I am male, I will have a long, thick mane around my head.

**14.** My name comes from the fact that I have eight tentacles. I like drifting silently across the sea floor.

**15.** I have an external skeleton. I live in the sea and scuttle sideways and I have two claws.

## GUESS THE REST: SCIENCE

The answer is given to each question below, but some of the letters are missing. Guess the rest of the letters correctly to make each answer complete.

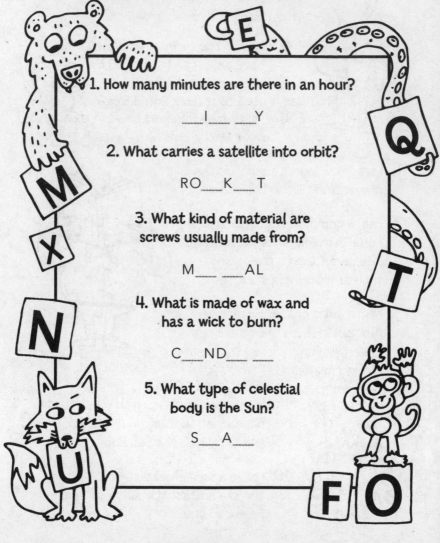

1. How many minutes are there in an hour?

___ I ___ ___ Y

2. What carries a satellite into orbit?

RO___ K___ T

3. What kind of material are screws usually made from?

M___ ___ AL

4. What is made of wax and has a wick to burn?

C___ ND___ ___

5. What type of celestial body is the Sun?

S___ A___

6. What does a battery supply?

___L___CT___ ___ ___I___Y

7. What gas is used to make a liquid fizzy?

C___RB___ ___ ___     D___OX___ ___E

8. What creates sound waves?

V___B___ ___T___ ___NS

9. What fluid does a mammal give to its young?

___I___K

10. What is the material in the middle of a pencil?

GR___PH___TE

# ODD ONE OUT: CLOTHING

Below are five lists. The words in each list relate to each other in some way, but there is an odd word out in each list that is not like the other three. Write the odd word out in the space below each list and also explain why.

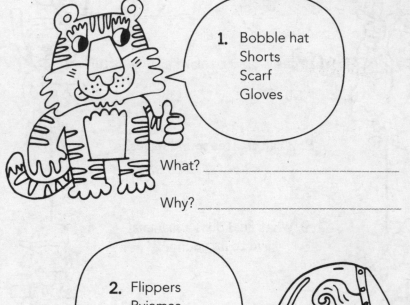

1. Bobble hat
   Shorts
   Scarf
   Gloves

What? _____

Why? _____

2. Flippers
   Pyjamas
   Snorkel
   Wetsuit

What? _____

Why? _____

**3.** Flip flops
   Skis
   Coat
   Salopettes

What? _____

Why? _____

**4.** Swimming hat
   Swimsuit
   Skirt
   Goggles

What? _____

Why? _____

**5.** Slippers
   Walking boots
   Football boots
   Cowboy boots

What? _____

Why? _____

## QUIZ SHOW: PREHISTORIC WORLD

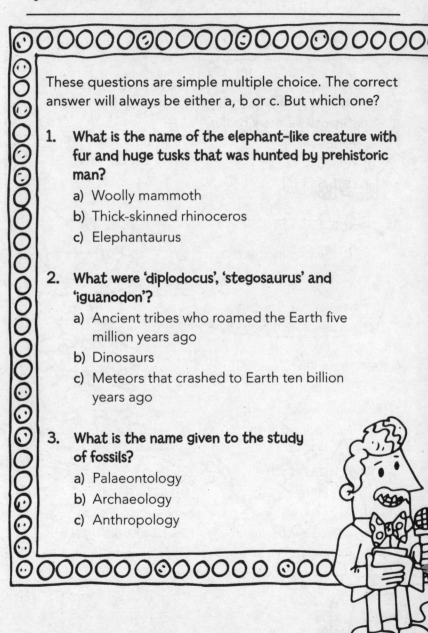

These questions are simple multiple choice. The correct answer will always be either a, b or c. But which one?

1. **What is the name of the elephant–like creature with fur and huge tusks that was hunted by prehistoric man?**
   a) Woolly mammoth
   b) Thick-skinned rhinoceros
   c) Elephantaurus

2. **What were 'diplodocus', 'stegosaurus' and 'iguanodon'?**
   a) Ancient tribes who roamed the Earth five million years ago
   b) Dinosaurs
   c) Meteors that crashed to Earth ten billion years ago

3. **What is the name given to the study of fossils?**
   a) Palaeontology
   b) Archaeology
   c) Anthropology

4.  **What was the name of the single giant landmass on Earth 200 million years ago that split to form the continents we know today?**
    a)  Pangaea
    b)  Atlantis
    c)  Ulysses

5.  **What is a fossil?**
    a)  An impression or cast of an animal or plant preserved within a rock
    b)  A dinosaur bone perfectly preserved in hardened tree sap
    c)  An ancient shell made from sandstone

6.  **Which of these dinosaurs was a carnivore?**
    a)  Triceratops
    b)  Tyrannosaurus rex
    c)  Diplodocus

7.  **What is a dodo?**
    a)  An extinct whale
    b)  An extinct bird
    c)  An extinct elephant

## MISSING WORDS: PLANTS

The sentences below each have a word missing. Pick the correct word from the box next to each sentence and write it in the space.

**1.** Acorns are the seeds of

_____ trees.

| Oak |
| Palm |
| Sycamore |

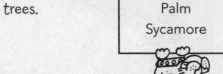

| Leaves |
| Flowers |
| Fruit |

**2.** Stamen, sepal, pistil and ovule are

all parts of _____.

**3.** Flowers have a sweet smell to

_____.

| Attract insects |
| Keep animals away |
| Release water |

| Apples |
| Potatoes |
| Carrots |

**4.** _____ grow on trees.

**5.** The sticky liquid in trees is called

_____.

Bark
Concentrate
Sap

Evergreen
Deciduous
Shedders

**6.** Trees that lose their leaves

in winter are called

_____.

**7.** The destruction of large forest

areas is called _____.

Deforestation
Stripping
Detreeing

Year rounders
Evergreen
Deciduous

**8.** Trees that keep their leaves

all year round are called

_____.

# TRUE OR FALSE: ANIMALS

Are the statements below true or false? Tick the box you think is correct.

**1. Snakes shed their skins because they get too hot in the summer.**

☐ 👍 True or false? 👎 ☐

**2. Bears never hibernate.**

☐ 👍 True or false? 👎 ☐

**3. Hippopotamuses are only found in Finland.**

☐ 👍 True or false? 👎 ☐

**4. Wool is often made from sheep hair.**

☐ 👍 True or false? 👎 ☐

**5. A scorpion's sting is at the end of its tail.**

☐ 👍 True or false? 👎 ☐

**6. A toucan is a reptile.**

☐ 👍 True or false? 👎 ☐

**7. A male horse is called a stallion.**

☐ 👍 True or false? 👎 ☐

**8. A rabbit's home is called a warren.**

☐ 👍 True or false? 👎 ☐

**9. A baby swan is called a tadpole.**

☐ 👍 True or false? 👎 ☐

**10. Zebras can change the colour of their stripes.**

☐ 👍 True or false? 👎 ☐

**11. The giraffe is the world's heaviest land animal.**

☐ 👍 True or false? 👎 ☐

**12. A female rabbit is called a doe.**

☐ 👍 True or false? 👎 ☐

**13. Penguins are capable of flight.**

☐ 👍 True or false? 👎 ☐

**14. An octopus has eight tentacles.**

☐ 👍 True or false? 👎 ☐

**15. A lion is a type of large cat.**

☐ 👍 True or false? 👎 ☐

# OUT OF ORDER: HISTORY

The words in the lists below are all in the wrong order.
Read the instructions above each list and then place the
words in the correct order by rewriting them in the spaces
on the right.

## 1. Place these US presidents by date of presidency, earliest first.

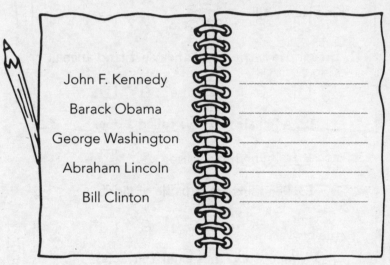

John F. Kennedy

Barack Obama

George Washington

Abraham Lincoln

Bill Clinton

_____

_____

_____

_____

_____

### 2. Place these kings and queens of England by date of reign, earliest first.

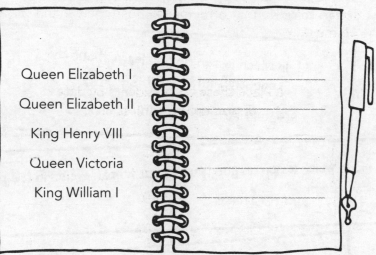

Queen Elizabeth I

Queen Elizabeth II

King Henry VIII

Queen Victoria

King William I

### 3. Place these famous battles by year, earliest first.

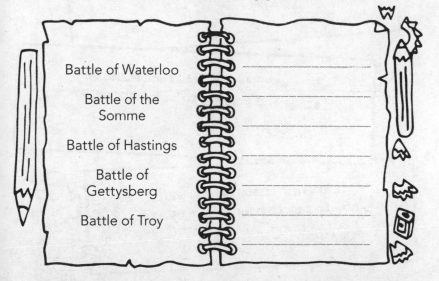

Battle of Waterloo

Battle of the Somme

Battle of Hastings

Battle of Gettysberg

Battle of Troy

# WORD JUMBLE: SCHOOL SUBJECTS

The answers are given to all these questions below. The only problem is that they're all jumbled up. Unjumble the letters to reveal the correct answer.

**1. In which lesson do you learn about the countries and features of Earth?**

RGGOPHAYE _____

**2. In which lesson do you learn about human events in the past?**

IRTYOSH _____

**3. In which lesson would you play sports?**

MAGSE _____

**4. In which lesson would you stand on a stage and pretend to be someone else?**

AMRDA _____

**5. In which lesson do you learn how to talk to people from Spain?**

SNAHIPS _____

# Quiz 15

Score...........................................

6. In which lesson do you learn to talk to people from France?

REFCHN _____

7. Which lesson involves addition, subtraction and division?

STEIMACHAMT _____

8. Which lesson includes biology, chemistry and physics?

SENCCEI _____

9. In which lesson do you learn how to paint and draw?

RTA _____

10. In which lesson do you learn to sing and play instruments?

UICSM _____

# MATCH UP: ANIMALS

Below are three sets of lists. Each word in the left-hand list can be matched up with a word in the right. Match all the words until they are all paired up.

## Match up these animals with their babies.

| | |
|---|---|
| Fish o | o Cub |
| Dog o | o Puppy |
| Rabbit o | o Kitten |
| Cat o | o Kit |
| Deer o | o Fawn |
| Cow o | o Calf |
| Hen o | o Chick |
| Goose o | o Fry |
| Tiger o | o Gosling |

**Match up these animal names with
the female names for that animal.**

| | |
|---|---|
| Bee o | o Vixen |
| Deer o | o Doe |
| Goat o | o Nanny goat |
| Fox o | o Queen |
| Chicken o | o Hen |
| Donkey o | o Sow |
| Sheep o | o Mare |
| Horse o | o Ewe |
| Pig o | o Jenny |

**Match up these animals with their habitats.**

| | |
|---|---|
| Giraffe o | o Ocean |
| Badger o | o Tree |
| Cow o | o Field |
| Frog o | o Pond |
| Bird o | o Woodland |
| Shark o | o Savannah |

# GUESS WHAT: HUMAN BODY

The sentences below all describe things relating to the human body. Try to guess what the answer is from the descriptions.

1. These are the two limbs on which you walk and stand.

2. These are the two limbs that connect to your shoulders.

3. These are the hard structures in your mouth, with which you bite and chew.

4. These organs enable you to see things. They each contain an iris and a lens.

5. These are part of your hands. You might wear rings on them.

6. This is the organ that pumps blood around the body.

7. This organ is inside your head and is the control centre of your body.

8. This is the framework of bones that supports your body.

9. These are the organs on either side of your head that allow you to hear.

**10.** These are the hard structures that grow at the tips of your fingers and toes.

**11.** This is the joint in the middle of your leg.

**12.** These are at the end of your legs. They have heels, toes and allow you to stand.

**13.** This grows from your head in many strands. You might often get it cut.

**14.** This is the organ in the middle of your face with which you smell and through which you breathe.

**15.** This is the waterproof covering over your whole body. It is the largest organ.

## GUESS THE REST: WHERE DO YOU GO?

The answer is given to each question below, but some of the letters are missing. Guess the rest of the letters correctly to make each answer complete.

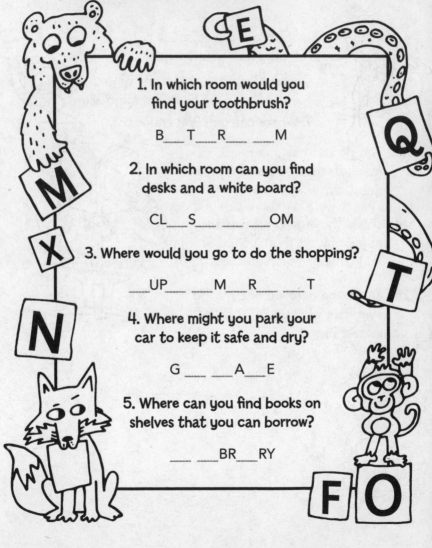

1. In which room would you find your toothbrush?

B_ T_ R_ _ _ M

2. In which room can you find desks and a white board?

CL_ _ S_ _ _ _ _ OM

3. Where would you go to do the shopping?

_ _ UP_ _ M_ R_ _ _ T

4. Where might you park your car to keep it safe and dry?

G_ _ _ _ A_ _ E

5. Where can you find books on shelves that you can borrow?

_ _ _ _ BR_ _ RY

## Quiz 18

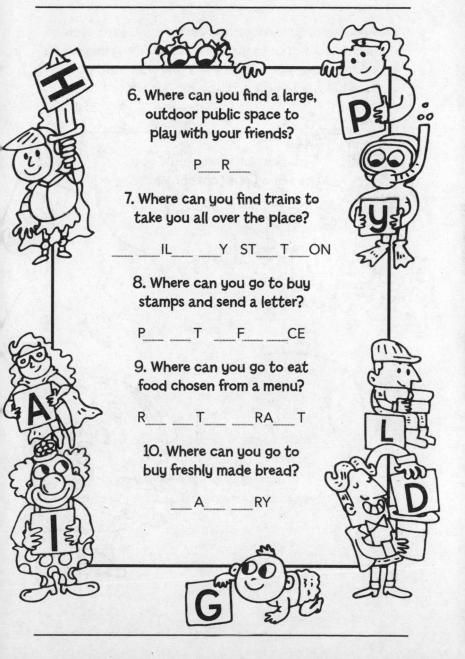

6. Where can you find a large, outdoor public space to play with your friends?

P__R____

7. Where can you find trains to take you all over the place?

___ ___IL___ ___Y ST___T__ON

8. Where can you go to buy stamps and send a letter?

P___ ___T ___F___ ___CE

9. Where can you go to eat food chosen from a menu?

R___ ___T___ ___RA___T

10. Where can you go to buy freshly made bread?

___A___ ___RY

# ODD ONE OUT: TRANSPORT

Below are five lists. The words in each list relate to each other in some way, but there is an odd word out in each list that is not like the other three. Write the odd word out in the space below each list and also explain why.

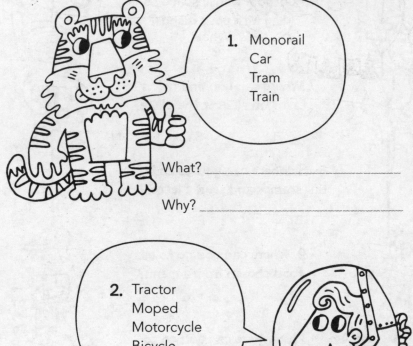

1. Monorail
   Car
   Tram
   Train

What? _____

Why? _____

2. Tractor
   Moped
   Motorcycle
   Bicycle

What? _____

Why? _____

**3.** Helicopter
Taxi
Hot-air balloon
Plane

What? _____

Why? _____

**4.** Bus
Dumper truck
Excavator
Bulldozer

What? _____

Why? _____

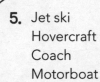

**5.** Jet ski
Hovercraft
Coach
Motorboat

What? _____

Why? _____

# QUIZ SHOW: MYTHS AND LEGENDS

These questions are simple multiple choice. The correct answer will always be either a, b or c. But which one?

1.  **Where is there rumoured to be a strange and monstrous aquatic creature in Scotland?**
    a) Caledonian Canal
    b) Loch Ness
    c) Firth of Forth

2.  **How many levels does the underworld have in Aztec mythology?**
    a) Nine
    b) Sixteen
    c) Three

3.  **How many eyes does a Cyclops have?**
    a) Two
    b) One
    c) Four

4.  **What kind of creature is a basilisk?**
    a) Monkey
    b) Lion
    c) Reptile

5.  **Who is the Greek god of the sea?**
    a) Poseidon
    b) Apollo
    c) Hermes

6.  **What happened to everything King Midas touched?**
    a) It turned to silver
    b) It turned to gold
    c) It turned to dust

7.  **What type of creature is a phoenix?**
    a) Bird
    b) Snake
    c) Dragon

## MISSING WORDS: BIRDS

The sentences below each have a word missing. Pick the correct word from the box next to each sentence and write it in the space.

1. The claw of a bird of prey is called a

_____.

Hook
Talon
Forcep

Penguin
Chicken
Swan

2. A _____ is a bird that is

not capable of flight.

3. A _____ goose is

called a gander.

Male
Female
Young

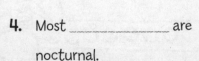

Eagles
Vultures
Owls

4. Most _____ are

nocturnal.

**5.** A young swan is called a

_____.

Cygnet
Swanlet
Crimp

Osprey
Albatross
Arctic tern

**6.** An _____ is the world's

largest seabird.

**7.** Ostriches originated in

_____.

India
Australia
Africa

Feathers
Wings
Beaks

**8.** Birds are the only animals with

_____.

# TRUE OR FALSE: SPACE

Are the statements below true or false? Tick the box you think is correct.

**1. The system of planets revolving around the Sun is called the Solar System.**

☐ 👍 True or false? 👎 ☐

**2. The Milky Way is a constellation in the night sky that gets its name from being shaped like a milk bottle.**

☐ 👍 True or false? 👎 ☐

**3. A lunar eclipse is caused by clouds obscuring the Moon.**

☐ 👍 True or false? 👎 ☐

**4. Saturn appears red in colour.**

☐ 👍 True or false? 👎 ☐

**5. Neptune is the hottest planet in our Solar System.**

☐ 👍 True or false? 👎 ☐

**6. A satellite is a celestial body or a man-made device that orbits around another celestial body, such as Earth.**

☐ 👍 True or false? 👎 ☐

**7. There are now thought to be eight planets in our Solar System.**

☐ 👍 True or false? 👎 ☐

8. An asteroid is a moon of Venus.

□ 👍 True or false? 👎 □

9. Venus is the closest planet to Earth.

□ 👍 True or false? 👎 □

10. In space, speed is measured in knots.

□ 👍 True or false? 👎 □

11. When the moon is less than half
visible, it is called a crescent.

□ 👍 True or false? 👎 □

12. Comets contain ice.

□ 👍 True or false? 👎 □

13. The Moon does not give off light.
It reflects light from the Sun.

□ 👍 True or false? 👎 □

14. Earth is the planet closest to the Sun.

□ 👍 True or false? 👎 □

15. A day on Earth is approximately 24 hours long.

□ 👍 True or false? 👎 □

## WORD JUMBLE: HOBBIES

The answers are given to all these questions below. The only problem is that they're all jumbled up. Unjumble the letters to reveal the correct answer.

1. What are you doing if you are looking at a book?

GRAIDNE _____

2. What is another word for a film?

OEIMV _____

3. What are you doing that involves two wheels and lots of pedalling?

YCCGINL _____

4. What are you doing that involves paper, pencils and colouring pencils?

RNDWAIG _____

5. What are you doing if you are flicking through the channels?

ACGIWNTH VT _____

6. What are you doing if you are heating something to eat in the kitchen?

GKCONOI _____

7. What are you doing if you are wearing headphones and tapping your feet?

EGTSINILN OT SCUMI _____

8. What are you doing if you are moving about to music?

CIDAGNN _____

9. What would you be doing if you were using a saddle, bridle and back protector?

HSEOR IIGDRN _____

10. What do you call it when friends come and stay the night?

SPELEORVE _____

# GUESS WHAT: EVERYDAY THINGS

The sentences below all describe everyday things. Try to guess what the answer is from the descriptions.

1. This is full of information about the world. You can read one every day and find out about current affairs. It is printed on paper.

2. These are worn on the feet when it's wet. You can splash in puddles and they will keep your feet dry.

3. This will shield you from the rain and bright sunlight. It can be carried around and be opened and closed.

4. When this is turned on it gives light. It can sit on a table or stand on a floor.

5. You go through this to get inside a house. Don't forget to lock it when you leave!

6. This is a container that carries people across water. It can have an engine or be powered with oars.

7. This is a kitchen appliance that boils water. It is very useful for making hot drinks.

8.  This is a flat rectangular invention on which you can watch moving pictures on different channels.

9.  This is driven on a road and carries a small number of people. It is powered by an engine.

10. This is an often sweet-smelling, colourful part of some plants. People often give bunches of these.

11. This sticky substance is used to bind things together. It comes in many different forms, such as in a liquid and in a stick.

12. This is a device easily carried around with you. It is used to contact other people and often can take photos as well.

13. This is a floppy, glossy book filled with photographs and articles to read.

14. This is a large shop where people go to buy food and household items regularly.

15. This hangs on the wall and tells you what time it is.

# ODD ONE OUT: SCHOOL

Below are five lists. The words in each list relate to each other in some way, but there is an odd word out in each list that is not like the other three. Write the odd word out in the space below each list and also explain why.

1.  History
    French
    German
    Spanish

What? _____

Why? _____

2.  Pencil
    Ballpoint pen
    Eraser
    Fountain pen

What? _____

Why? _____

**3.** Pencil sharpener
Ruler
Compass
Protractor

What? _____

Why? _____

**4.** Paintbrushes
Pencils
Calculator
Paints

What? _____

Why? _____

**5.** Teacher
Janitor
Cafeteria staff
Pupils

What? _____

Why? _____

# LEVEL ONE:
## What's your score?

Quiz 1 ..........
Quiz 2 ..........
Quiz 3 ..........
Quiz 4 ..........
Quiz 5 ..........
Quiz 6 ..........
Quiz 7 ..........
Quiz 8 ..........
Quiz 9 ..........
Quiz 10 ..........
Quiz 11 ..........
Quiz 12 ..........
Quiz 13 ..........

Quiz 14 ..........
Quiz 15 ..........
Quiz 16 ..........
Quiz 17 ..........
Quiz 18 ..........
Quiz 19 ..........
Quiz 20 ..........
Quiz 21 ..........
Quiz 22 ..........
Quiz 23 ..........
Quiz 24 ..........
Quiz 25 ..........

Grand total ..............

LEVEL
TWO

## QUIZ SHOW: HUMAN BODY

These questions are simple multiple choice. The correct answer will always be either a, b or c. But which one?

1.  **What makes blood circulate around the body?**
    a) It flows from your lungs when you breathe
    b) The movement of your body
    c) It is pumped round by your heart

2.  **What are triceps and biceps?**
    a) Arm muscles
    b) Leg muscles
    c) Arm bones

3.  **Where are the bones called humerus, radius and ulna found?**
    a) Leg
    b) Arm
    c) Foot

4.  **How many sweat glands do humans have?**
    a) Two million
    b) One thousand
    c) One hundred

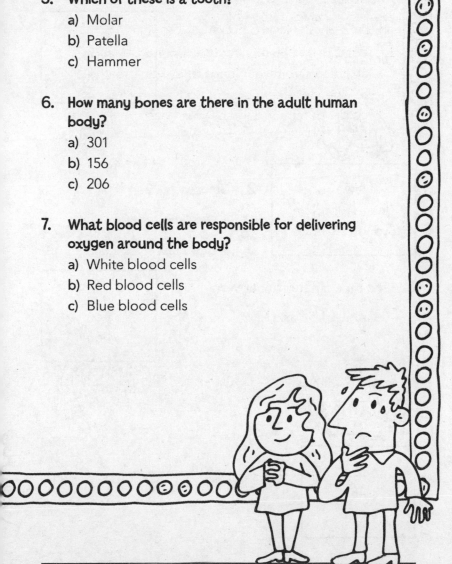

5. **Which of these is a tooth?**
   a) Molar
   b) Patella
   c) Hammer

6. **How many bones are there in the adult human body?**
   a) 301
   b) 156
   c) 206

7. **What blood cells are responsible for delivering oxygen around the body?**
   a) White blood cells
   b) Red blood cells
   c) Blue blood cells

## MISSING WORDS: TIME

The sentences below each have a word missing. Pick the correct word from the box next to each sentence and write it in the space.

1.  In the 24-hour clock, 8.30 pm is

    written as _____.

    20:30
    18:30
    21:20

New York
United Kingdom
Sydney, Australia

2.  Greenwich Mean Time

    is the time zone of

    _____.

3.  The time difference between

    California, USA and New York, USA,

    is _____.

    8 hours
    5 hours
    3 hours

52
48
66

4.  There are _____ weeks in

    a year.

**5.** A _____ is an instrument that uses sunlight to tell the time.

Sun clock
Sundial
Light-metre

Sun-year
Light-year
Light-leap

**6.** A _____ is the distance travelled by light in a vacuum in one year.

**7.** The science of time measurement is called _____.

Chromatics
Horology
Optics

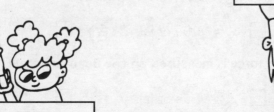

Nanosecond
Millisecond
Jiffy

**8.** A _____ is one billionth of a second.

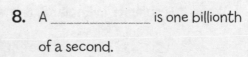

# TRUE OR FALSE?: NATURAL WORLD

Are the statements below true or false? Tick the box you think is correct.

**1. Sea water is heavier than fresh water because it contains salt.**

☐ 👍 True or false? 👎 ☐

**2. Oxygen is mainly formed by volcanic eruptions.**

☐ 👍 True or false? 👎 ☐

**3. Water is a liquid compound of oxygen and helium.**

☐ 👍 True or false? 👎 ☐

**4. An animal or plant vulnerable to extinction is said to be 'endangered'.**

☐ 👍 True or false? 👎 ☐

**5. Gravity is the force that enables objects to travel upwards.**

☐ 👍 True or false? 👎 ☐

**6. Wind force is measured on the Beaufort scale.**

☐ 👍 True or false? 👎 ☐

**7. When it is summer in England, it is winter in Australia.**

☐ 👍 True or false? 👎 ☐

8. Winds are caused by the gravitational pull of the Moon.

☐  True or false?  ☐

9. Paper is made from water and crushed oyster shells.

☐  True or false?  ☐

10. Sapphires are famously blue in colour.

☐  True or false?  ☐

11. Tides are caused by excessive rainfall.

☐  True or false?  ☐

12. Coral is formed from the skeletons of sea creatures.

☐  True or false?  ☐

13. Pearls are mined from quarries.

☐  True or false?  ☐

14. The aurora borealis is a ring that appears
around the Moon at certain times of year.

☐  True or false?  ☐

15. The molten rock that flows
from a volcano is called 'lava'.

☐  True or false?  ☐

# OUT OF ORDER: SPACE

The words in the lists below are all in the wrong order. Read the instructions above each list and then place the words in the correct order by rewriting them in the spaces on the right.

## 1. Place these planets by distance to the Sun, closest first.

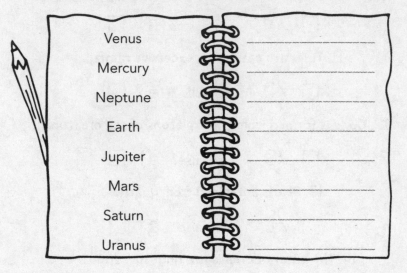

Venus _____

Mercury _____

Neptune _____

Earth _____

Jupiter _____

Mars _____

Saturn _____

Uranus _____

**2. Place these phases of the Moon in order, starting with the New Moon and getting fuller.**

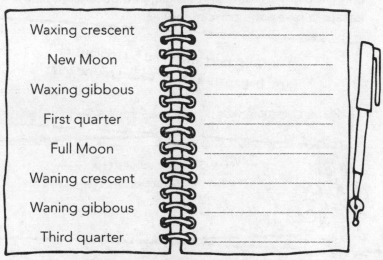

Waxing crescent

New Moon

Waxing gibbous

First quarter

Full Moon

Waning crescent

Waning gibbous

Third quarter

**3. Place these planets by length of time to rotate once, shortest first.**

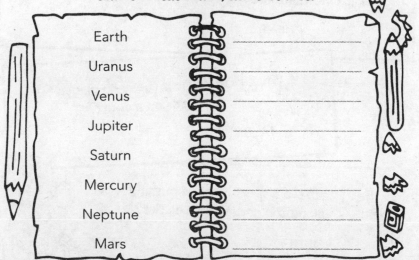

Earth

Uranus

Venus

Jupiter

Saturn

Mercury

Neptune

Mars

## WORD JUMBLE: SPORTS

The answers are given to all these questions below. The only problem is that they're all jumbled up. Unjumble the letters to reveal the correct answer.

**1. Which sport, followed by millions of fans, began as a game called rounders?**

SLEBALAB _____

**2. What game involves the terms bowler, wicket keeper and wicket?**

KECRICT _____

**3. As well as American Football and Australian Rules Football, which international sport is played with an oval ball?**

BUGYR _____

**4. What team game is typically played by fourteen girls on a court?**

TALBNEL _____

**5. What team sport involves pushing a ball along the ground with a stick?**

YOCHEK _____

6. Which sport uses skates to move in a dance-like way across a layer of frozen water?

EIC TISKANG

_____

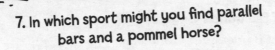

7. In which sport might you find parallel bars and a pommel horse?

NISTASCMGY

_____

8. In which sport are there strokes named butterfly and freestyle?

MIMNSWIG

_____

9. Which city hosted the Olympics in 2008?

JBIEING

_____

10. Doing gymnastics on a sprung surface is called what?

PAMINGORLTIN

_____

## HALL OF FAME: GEOGRAPHY

The multiple-choice questions below are all things that deserve a place in a hall of fame. Test your knowledge on the world's biggest, brightest and best.

1. **What is the world's largest country in the world by area?**
   a. Russia
   b. Chile
   c. Japan

2. **What is the world's longest reef?**
   a. Great Barrier Reef, Coral Sea
   b. Red Sea Coral Reef, Red Sea
   c. New Caledonia Barrier Reef, Pacific Ocean

3. **Which is the world's largest continent?**
   a. Europe
   b. Africa
   c. Asia

4. **What is the world's biggest hot desert?**
   a. Gobi
   b. Sahara
   c. Arabian

5. **What is the world's highest mountain?**
   a. K2
   b. Mount Everest
   c. Mount Sinai

6.  **What is the world's biggest ocean?**
    a. Atlantic ocean
    b. Indian ocean
    c. Pacific ocean

7.  **Where is the deepest place on Earth?**
    a. Mariana Trench
    b. Puerto Rico Trench
    c. Tonga Trench

8.  **Which two countries have the greatest number of neighbouring countries touching their borders?**
    a. Germany and Poland
    b. China and Russia
    c. USA and Canada

9.  **What is the hardest natural mineral on Earth?**
    a. Ruby
    b. Granite
    c. Diamond

10. **What is the largest country in South America by area?**
    a. Brazil
    b. Argentina
    c. Bolivia

## MATCH UP: COUNTRIES

Below are three sets of lists. Each word in the left-hand list can be matched up with a word in the right. Match all the words until they are all paired up.

### Match up these US cities with their state.

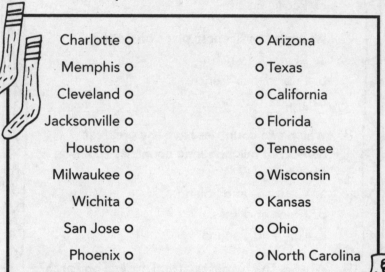

Charlotte o

Memphis o

Cleveland o

Jacksonville o

Houston o

Milwaukee o

Wichita o

San Jose o

Phoenix o

o Arizona

o Texas

o California

o Florida

o Tennessee

o Wisconsin

o Kansas

o Ohio

o North Carolina

# Quiz 32

## Match up the countries with their currencies.

Lira o      o Japan

Ruble o      o Switzerland

Krona o      o Sweden

Franc o      o Russia

Dollar o      o Singapore

Yen o      o Turkey

Euro o      o Mexico

Yuan o      o China

Peso o      o France

## Match up the countries that border each other.

Colombia o      o Poland

Morocco o      o Mongolia

Argentina o      o Algeria

Norway o      o Sweden

China o      o Chile

Germany o      o Peru

## GUESS WHAT: OCCUPATIONS

The sentences below all describe different jobs. Try to guess what the answer is from the description.

1. I drive metal carriages on tracks that carry people from one place to another.

2. I walk the streets of towns and cities to make sure they are safe. I stop anyone carrying out crime.

3. I work in a team with others to create structures that people can use.

4. I move around a stage to music in front of an audience.

5. I have to pretend to be other people and make audiences believe the story I am telling them.

6. I use my pen or keyboard to create different worlds and characters to scare, move and delight people.

7. I work in big financial corporations that manage money for customers.

8. I am very creative. I might sculpt, paint or photograph my creations.

9. I am good at helping other people learn information and study skills.

10. I work outdoors with plants and flowers. I work in areas from backyards to great parks.

11. I use my voice at different pitches to perform a piece of music.

12. I look after a wide range of animals, often ones that are endangered. I feed them and make sure their homes are clean.

13. I work in a restaurant, taking orders and bringing customers their food and drinks.

14. I kick a ball around a field with my team mates and aim to get it into the back of a net.

15. I carry people through the air in a flying machine and take them all over the world.

## GUESS THE REST: ANIMALS

The answer is given to each question below, but some of the letters are missing. Guess the rest of the letters correctly to make each answer complete.

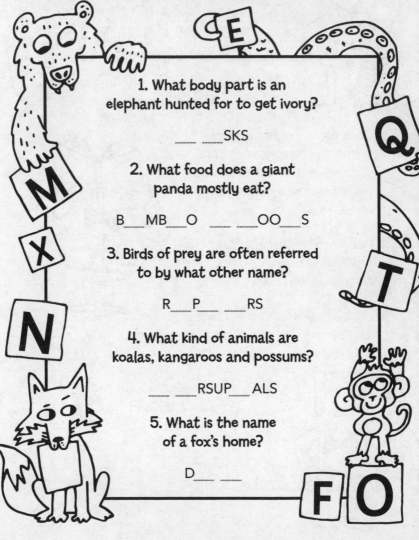

1. What body part is an elephant hunted for to get ivory?

___ ___SKS

2. What food does a giant panda mostly eat?

B__MB__O ___ ___OO___S

3. Birds of prey are often referred to by what other name?

R__P___ ___RS

4. What kind of animals are koalas, kangaroos and possums?

___ ___RSUP___ALS

5. What is the name of a fox's home?

D___ ___

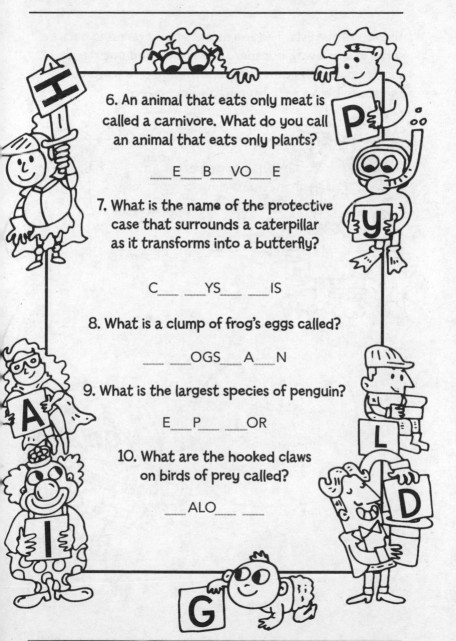

6. An animal that eats only meat is called a carnivore. What do you call an animal that eats only plants?

\_\_\_ E \_\_ B \_ VO \_\_\_ E

7. What is the name of the protective case that surrounds a caterpillar as it transforms into a butterfly?

C \_\_\_ \_\_\_ YS \_\_\_ \_\_\_ IS

8. What is a clump of frog's eggs called?

\_\_\_ \_\_\_ OGS \_\_\_ A \_\_ N

9. What is the largest species of penguin?

E \_\_\_ P \_\_\_ \_\_\_ OR

10. What are the hooked claws on birds of prey called?

\_\_\_ \_\_\_ ALO \_\_\_ \_\_ \_\_

# ODD ONE OUT: MUSICAL INSTRUMENTS

Below are five lists. The words in each list relate to each other in some way, but there is an odd word out in each list that is not like the other three. Write the odd word out in the space below each list and also explain why.

1. Timpani
   Kettle
   Bongo
   French horn

What? _____

Why? _____

2. Wooden
   Woodwind
   Brass
   String

What? _____

Why? _____

**Quiz 35**

**3.** Violin
Cello
Cymbals
Double bass

What? _____

Why? _____

**4.** Sitar
Bongo
Electric guitar
Banjo

What? _____

Why? _____

**5.** Tuba
Clarinet
Flute
Oboe

What? _____

Why? _____

## QUIZ SHOW: NUMBERS

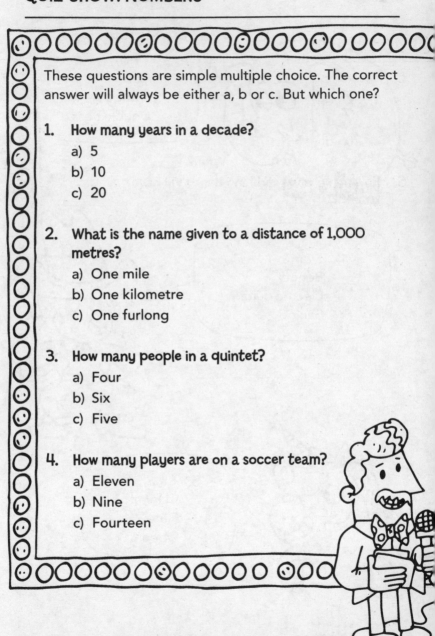

These questions are simple multiple choice. The correct answer will always be either a, b or c. But which one?

1.  **How many years in a decade?**
    a) 5
    b) 10
    c) 20

2.  **What is the name given to a distance of 1,000 metres?**
    a) One mile
    b) One kilometre
    c) One furlong

3.  **How many people in a quintet?**
    a) Four
    b) Six
    c) Five

4.  **How many players are on a soccer team?**
    a) Eleven
    b) Nine
    c) Fourteen

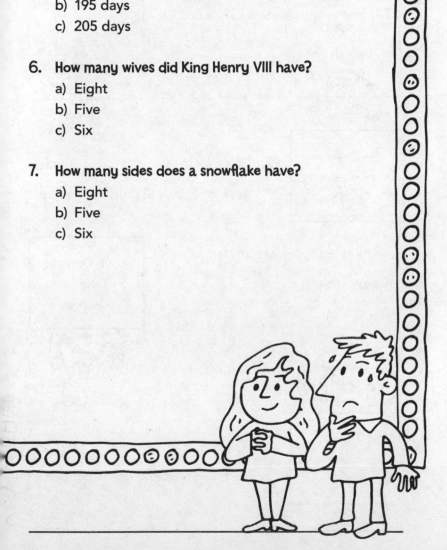

5.  How long is a year on Venus?
    a) 225 days
    b) 195 days
    c) 205 days

6.  How many wives did King Henry VIII have?
    a) Eight
    b) Five
    c) Six

7.  How many sides does a snowflake have?
    a) Eight
    b) Five
    c) Six

## MISSING WORDS: COLOURS

The sentences below each have a word missing. Pick the correct word from the box next to each sentence and write it in the space.

**1.** There are _____ colours in a rainbow.

Seven
Six
Five

Red
Green
Orange

**2.** The colour _____ is made by mixing blue and yellow pigment

**3.** The primary colours are red, blue and _____.

Yellow
Green
Orange

Blue
White
Orange

**4.** The colour _____ is made by mixing red and yellow pigment.

**5.** The light band consisting of all colours is called a _____.

Lightshow
Radiograph
Spectrum

Yellow
Blue
White

**6.** We see a rainbow when _____ light passes through a prism and splits up.

**7.** The sky is blue because blue _____ is scattered more than other colours by the atmosphere.

Gas
Light
Clouds

Shorter than
Longer than
The same length as

**8.** Blue light wavelengths are

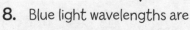

red light wavelengths.

# TRUE OR FALSE: GEOGRAPHY

Are the statements below true or false? Tick the box you think is correct.

### 1. Lisbon is the capital of Portugal.

☐ 👍 True or false? 👎 ☐

### 2. Chicago is a city in Australia.

☐ 👍 True or false? 👎 ☐

### 3. Kenya is on the continent of Africa.

☐ 👍 True or false? 👎 ☐

### 4. Corsica is a French island in the Mediterranean Sea.

☐ 👍 True or false? 👎 ☐

### 5. 'Victoria' is a lake in Africa.

☐ 👍 True or false? 👎 ☐

### 6. Cape Town is in New Zealand.

☐ 👍 True or false? 👎 ☐

### 7. The huge body of water that lies between Europe and North America is called the Atlantic Ocean.

☐ 👍 True or false? 👎 ☐

8. The Thames is a river that flows through London, England.

☐ 👍 True or false? 👎 ☐

9. Mount Etna is in Hawaii.

☐ 👍 True or false? 👎 ☐

10. Nigeria is a country in South America.

☐ 👍 True or false? 👎 ☐

11. The vast region in Asia called the Gobi is mainly grassland.

☐ 👍 True or false? 👎 ☐

12. Pakistan is not in Europe.

☐ 👍 True or false? 👎 ☐

13. The Panama Canal in Central America
links the Atlantic and Pacific Oceans.

☐ 👍 True or false? 👎 ☐

14. The Great Barrier Reef is off the west coast of Scotland.

☐ 👍 True or false? 👎 ☐

15. New Zealand consists of two main islands
called the North Island and the South Island.

☐ 👍 True or false? 👎 ☐

# OUT OF ORDER: NUMBERS

The words in the lists below are all in the wrong order.
Read the instructions above each list and then place the
words in the correct order by rewriting them in the spaces
on the right.

### 1. Place these Roman numerals in increasing order.

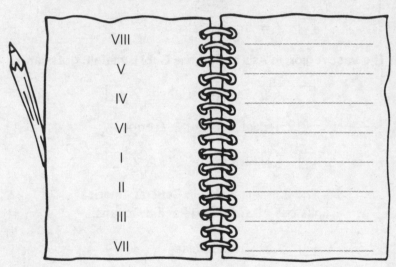

VIII

V

IV

VI

I

II

III

VII

### 2. Place these bytes by size, smallest first.

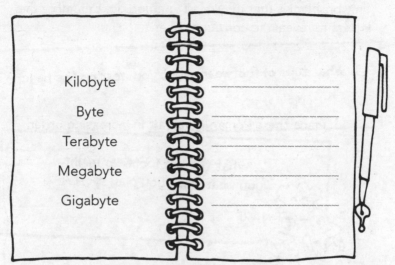

Kilobyte        _____

Byte            _____

Terabyte        _____

Megabyte        _____

Gigabyte        _____

### 3. Place these shapes by number of sides, smallest number first.

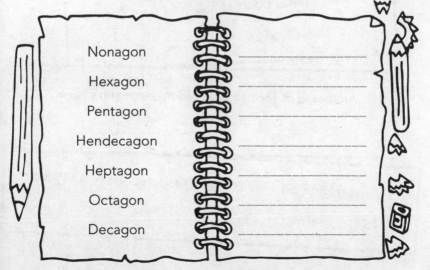

Nonagon         _____

Hexagon         _____

Pentagon        _____

Hendecagon      _____

Heptagon        _____

Octagon         _____

Decagon         _____

# WORD JUMBLE: FOOTWEAR

The answers are given to all these questions below. The only problem is that they're all jumbled up. Unjumble the letters to reveal the correct answer.

**1. What type of footwear might you wear on the beach?**

LPIF FPLSO _____

**2. What type of footwear might you wear when you play sport?**

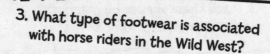

NARRTISE _____

**3. What type of footwear is associated with horse riders in the Wild West?**

OCOYBW OBSTO _____

**4. What kind of footwear would make wearers taller?**

IGHH ELESH _____

**5. What might you wear to walk through puddles and mud?**

NOTELLINGW OTOBS _____

### 6. What might you wear on your feet before going to bed?

RPSELSIP       _____

### 7. What do scuba divers wear on their feet so they can swim faster?

PIRPFSLE       _____

### 8. What do some dancers wear on their feet?

TLBLEA SESHO       _____

### 9. What might you wear on your feet when you go hiking?

GWKNLIA TOSBO       _____

### 10. What type of shoes were traditionally made out of wood?

SLOGC       _____

## HALL OF FAME: COUNTRIES

The multiple-choice questions below are all things that deserve a place in a hall of fame. Test your knowledge on the world's biggest, brightest and best.

1. **Which country has the largest population?**
   a. Japan
   b. USA
   c. China

2. **Which is the smallest continent?**
   a. Australia
   b. Europe
   c. North America

3. **Which is the only continent which has no indigenous population?**
   a. Australia
   b. Antarctica
   c. North America

4. **Which capital city has the largest population?**
   a. Beijing, China
   b. Cairo, Egypt
   c. Madrid, Spain

5. **Which country is the biggest producer of cotton?**
   a. China
   b. Australia
   c. Brazil

6. **Milan is the largest city in which country?**
   a. Italy
   b. France
   c. Austria

7. **What is the largest country in North America?**
   a. USA
   b. Mexico
   c. Canada

8. **Which country produces the most cheese?**
   a. Switzerland
   b. Argentina
   c. France

9. **Which country has the longest coastline?**
   a. Australia
   b. South Africa
   c. Canada

10. **What is the world's smallest country?**
   a. Liechtenstein
   b. Vatican City
   c. Malta

# MATCH UP: ANIMALS

Below are three sets of lists. Each word in the left-hand list can be matched up with a word in the right. Match all the words until they are all paired up.

## Match up the features with the animal.

| | |
|---|---|
| Fangs o | o Rabbit |
| Talons o | o Eagle |
| Flippers o | o Fish |
| Fur o | o Snake |
| Mane o | o Horse |
| Hands o | o Duck |
| Tusks o | o Elephant |
| Scales o | o Pig |
| Snout o | o Penguin |
| Bill o | o Chimpanzee |

## Match up these animals with their group name.

| | |
|---|---|
| Wolves o | o Swarm |
| Gorillas o | o Herd |
| Dolphins o | o Flock |
| Puppies o | o Pack |
| Bees o | o Litter |
| Geese o | o Pod |
| Lions o | o Pride |
| Cows o | o Band |

 **Match these animals with their calls.**

| | |
|---|---|
| Cow o | o Bark |
| Horse o | o Meeow |
| Wolf o | o Hoot |
| Cat o | o Neigh |
| Duck o | o Bleat |
| Owl o | o Moo |
| Sheep o | o Howl |
| Lion o | o Roar |
| Dog o | o Quack |

## GUESS WHAT: FOOD

The sentences below all describe foods. Try to guess what the answer is from the descriptions.

1. This is a small grain eaten all over the world. It likes to grow in wet conditions. It is very popular with curry.

2. This is very popular in Italy. It is long and thin and you eat it covered in a tomato sauce.

3. This is a hard or soft creamy food that is made from the curds of milk.

4. This is a large green fruit with watery red flesh inside.

5. This is a salad vegetable. It has layers of leaves. Some examples of types are iceberg and romaine.

6. These are small green vegetables. They grow in pods.

7. This has a hard outer shell and has white flesh inside. It contains very nutritious milk and grows in hot places.

8. This is an edible plant that grows in the ground. It can be mashed, baked or made into crisps or chips.

**9.** These are either red or green or black. They grow on vines. They are crushed and fermented to make wine.

**10.** This is very cold and comes in many different flavours, such as strawberry or chocolate. It was invented in China as early as 3000 BC.

**11.** This is a sweet treat made from cacao beans. It can be in a solid bar, a sauce, or hot and drinkable.

**12.** This is a very popular tomato sauce that can be eaten on chips or on a hotdog.

**13.** This popular dish has a flat, bread-like base and can have many different toppings. It was invented in Naples, Italy, but became famous in the USA.

**14.** This is a long, curved yellow fruit that gets brown spots as it ripens.

**15.** This is a big type of squash that is common around the time of Halloween. People dig out the insides and carve a face on to it.

## GUESS THE REST: WORDS

The answer is given to each question below, but some of the letters are missing. Guess the rest of the letters correctly to make each answer complete.

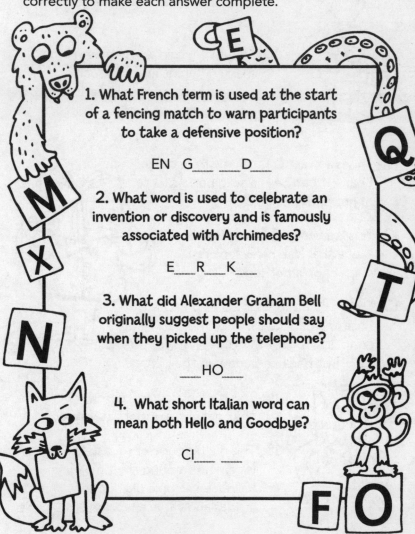

1. What French term is used at the start of a fencing match to warn participants to take a defensive position?

EN  G___  ___D___

2. What word is used to celebrate an invention or discovery and is famously associated with Archimedes?

E_ _R_ _K___

3. What did Alexander Graham Bell originally suggest people should say when they picked up the telephone?

___HO___

4. What short Italian word can mean both Hello and Goodbye?

CI___  ___

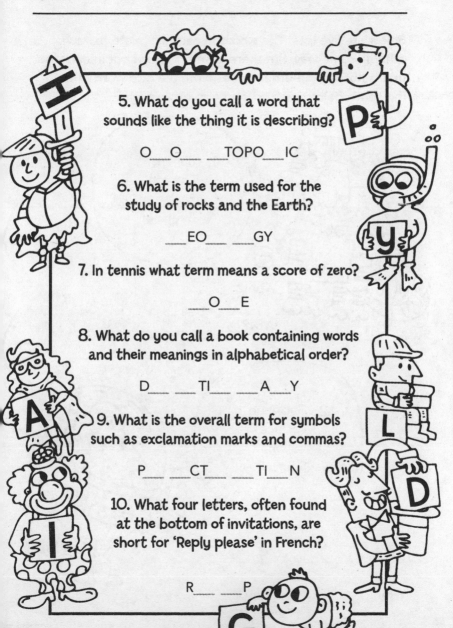

5. What do you call a word that sounds like the thing it is describing?

O__O____ TOPO___IC

6. What is the term used for the study of rocks and the Earth?

____EO____ __GY

7. In tennis what term means a score of zero?

___O__E

8. What do you call a book containing words and their meanings in alphabetical order?

D___ ___TI___ ___A___Y

9. What is the overall term for symbols such as exclamation marks and commas?

P___ ___CT ___ ___TI___N

10. What four letters, often found at the bottom of invitations, are short for 'Reply please' in French?

R___ ___P

# ODD ONE OUT: FOOD

Below are five lists. The words in each list relate to each other in some way, but there is an odd word out in each list that is not like the other three. Write the odd word out in the space below each list and also explain why.

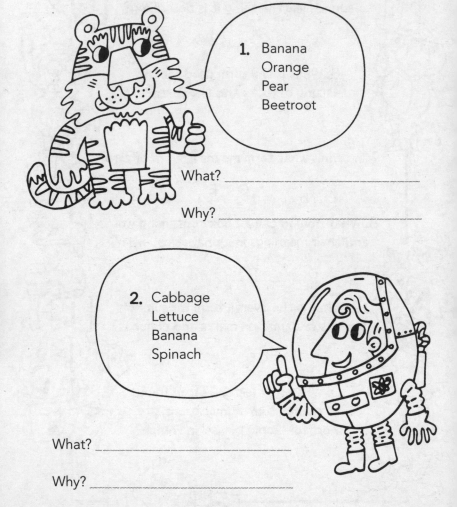

1. Banana
   Orange
   Pear
   Beetroot

What? _____

Why? _____

2. Cabbage
   Lettuce
   Banana
   Spinach

What? _____

Why? _____

**3.** Mushroom
Turnip
Sweet potato
Yam

What? _____

Why? _____

**4.** Blueberry
Apple
Gooseberry
Cranberry

What? _____

Why? _____

**5.** Peanut
Pecan
Fig
Almond

What? _____

Why? _____

# QUIZ SHOW: ENVIRONMENT

These questions are simple multiple choice. The correct answer will always be either a, b or c. But which one?

1. **Which of these winds is strongest?**
   a) Gale
   b) Hurricane
   c) Breeze

2. **What causes wind?**
   a) Differences in air pressure
   b) Differences in sky colour
   c) Differences in the sea temperature

3. **What is bamboo?**
   a) A tree
   b) A root vegetable
   c) A grass

4.  **What is the name for the imaginary great circle that passes around the Earth, at equal distance from the North and South Pole?**
    a) The equilibrium
    b) The Earth line
    c) The equator

5.  **What is the name for a group of mountains?**
    a) Chain
    b) Range
    c) String

6.  **When the tide 'ebbs' what is happening to it?**
    a) It's coming in
    b) It's staying constant
    c) It's going out

7.  **What makes Uluru (Ayers Rock) in Australia red?**
    a) Minerals
    b) Algae growing on the surface
    c) Reaction to sunlight

# MISSING WORDS: SOUND

The sentences below each have a word missing. Pick the correct word from the box next to each sentence and write it in the space.

1. When sound bounces back from an

   obstacle, we hear _____.

   > An echo
   > A hum
   > A bang

   > Materials
   > Textures
   > Tensions

2. The strings of a harp each produce a

   different sound because they are of

   varying lengths and _____.

3. A _____ produces sound

   when strings are hit by wooden

   hammers.

   > Cello
   > Piano
   > Accordion

   > Eardrum
   > Earlobe
   > Gavel

4. The _____ is a thin flap

   of skin in the ear that vibrates

   when sounds hit it.

**5.** Sound is measured in

_____.

Decibels
Volts
Calories

A brick wall
A vacuum
Carbon fibre

**6.** Sound cannot travel through

_____.

**7.** If someone is deaf, they

might communicate with

_____.

Braille
Morse code
Sign language

Gets higher
Gets lower
Stays the same

**8.** As you tighten a drum skin, the

sound made when you hit it

_____ in pitch.

# TRUE OR FALSE: WATER

Are the statements below true or false? Tick the box you think is correct.

### 1. A pumpkin is about 90 per cent water.

☐ 👍 True or false? 👎 ☐

### 2. The Red Sea gets its name from the high salt content that turns its water red.

☐ 👍 True or false? 👎 ☐

### 3. When underwater, frogs breathe through their skin.

☐ 👍 True or false? 👎 ☐

### 4. There is a large ocean on Jupiter.

☐ 👍 True or false? 👎 ☐

### 5. A camel stores water in its hump.

☐ 👍 True or false? 👎 ☐

### 6. Water waves are caused by the wind blowing over the surface of the water.

☐ 👍 True or false? 👎 ☐

### 7. A submarine sinks by taking in water.

☐ 👍 True or false? 👎 ☐

**8. Brussels is divided in two by the River Rhine.**

☐ 👍 True or false? 👎 ☐

**9. Over 70 per cent of Earth's surface is covered by water.**

☐ 👍 True or false? 👎 ☐

**10. A glacier is a mountain lake containing very cold water.**

☐ 👍 True or false? 👎 ☐

**11. Hydroelectricity is electricity produced by using flowing water.**

☐ 👍 True or false? 👎 ☐

**12. The Greenland Sea is in the Arctic Ocean.**

☐ 👍 True or false? 👎 ☐

**13. The city of Venice is built on small islands separated by canals and linked by bridges.**

☐ 👍 True or false? 👎 ☐

**14. The Congo River is the world's longest river.**

☐ 👍 True or false? 👎 ☐

**15. Over 40 per cent of the Earth's water is contained in the Caspian Sea.**

☐ 👍 True or false? 👎 ☐

# OUT OF ORDER: GEOGRAPHY

The words in the lists below are all in the wrong order. Read the instructions above each list and then place the words in the correct order by rewriting them in the spaces on the right.

## 1. Place these rivers by length, longest first.

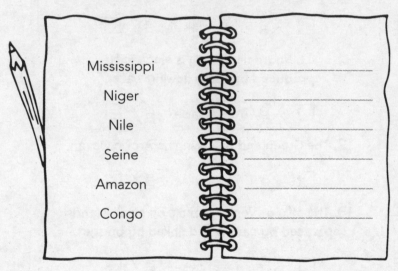

Mississippi

Niger

Nile

Seine

Amazon

Congo

_____

_____

_____

_____

_____

_____

### 2. Place these oceans by size, largest first.

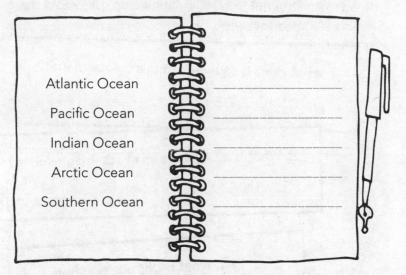

Atlantic Ocean

Pacific Ocean

Indian Ocean

Arctic Ocean

Southern Ocean

### 3. Place these mountains by height, tallest first.

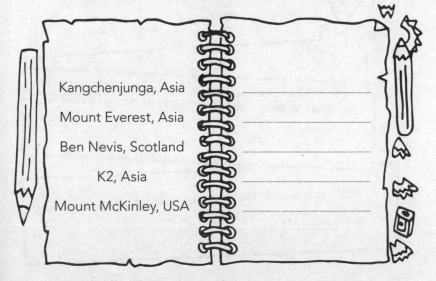

Kangchenjunga, Asia

Mount Everest, Asia

Ben Nevis, Scotland

K2, Asia

Mount McKinley, USA

# WORD JUMBLE: FOOD AND DRINK

The answers are given to all these questions below. The only problem is that they're all jumbled up. Unjumble the letters to reveal the correct answer.

1. What drink is squeezed from a colourful fruit?

RAONEG CIUJE _____

2. What is a Chinese dish of stir-fried noodles?

WHOC EMNI _____

3. What might you buy from some fast-food restaurants?

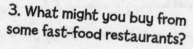

EHCESE EGRBUR _____

4. What is very cold and comes in many flavours?

CEI EMCRA _____

5. What is a sweet, thick drink made of blended fruit?

SOMOIETH _____

6. What is the name of a popular dessert made up of a fruit and pastry?

LPEPA EPI

7. What is dark and sticky and covered in yummy icing?

LCECATHOO ECKA

8. What is the name of a long, thin kind of pasta, often served with a Bolognese sauce?

PIGHATSET

9. Which yellow fruit is high in the chemical element potassium?

ABNAAN

10. What dairy food is France famous for producing?

EEHCES

# HALL OF FAME: ANIMALS

The multiple-choice questions below are all things that deserve a place in a hall of fame. Test your knowledge on the world's biggest, brightest and best.

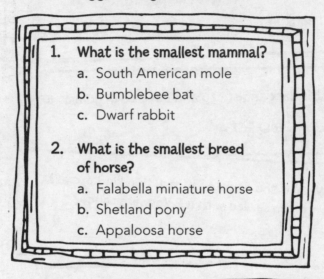

1.  **What is the smallest mammal?**
    a.  South American mole
    b.  Bumblebee bat
    c.  Dwarf rabbit

2.  **What is the smallest breed of horse?**
    a.  Falabella miniature horse
    b.  Shetland pony
    c.  Appaloosa horse

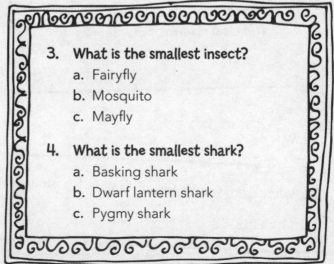

3.  **What is the smallest insect?**
    a.  Fairyfly
    b.  Mosquito
    c.  Mayfly

4.  **What is the smallest shark?**
    a.  Basking shark
    b.  Dwarf lantern shark
    c.  Pygmy shark

5. **What is the smallest bird?**
   a. Lorikeet
   b. Goldfinch
   c. Bee hummingbird

6. **What is the smallest reptile?**
   a. Diamondback terrapin
   b. Dwarf gecko
   c. Milk snake

7. **What is the slowest-moving reptile?**
   a. Hermann's tortoise
   b. Giant Galapagos tortoise
   c. Dwarf crocodile

8. **What is the smallest breed of dog?**
   a. Chihuahua
   b. Papillon
   c. Chinese crested

9. **What is the smallest breed of cat?**
   a. Ragdoll
   b. Siamese
   c. Singapura

10. **What is the slowest-flying bird?**
    a. Red kite
    b. American woodcock
    c. Japanese wood pigeon

# MATCH UP: SPORTS

Below are three sets of lists. Each word in the left-hand list can be matched up with a word in the right. Match all the words until they are all paired up.

## Match up the equipment with the right sport.

| | |
|---|---|
| Shuttlecock o | o Tennis |
| Bow and arrow o | o Relay |
| Baton o | o Archery |
| Racket o | o Badminton |
| Padded gloves o | o Football |
| Wicket o | o Golf |
| Shin pads o | o Boxing |
| Mat o | o Skiing |
| Club o | o Cricket |
| Poles o | o Yoga |

## Quiz 52

Score........................................

### Match up the football team with its country.

Los Angeles Galaxy o     o England

Fluminense o     o Spain

Bayern Munich o     o Italy

Manchester United o     o Germany

Juventus o     o USA

Real Madrid o     o Brazil

### Match up the sports with where they take place.

Football o     o Pool

Baseball o     o Pitch

Ping pong o     o Court

Ice hockey o     o Course

Tennis o     o Table

Bowling o     o Field

Golf o     o Rink

Swimming o     o Alley

# GUESS WHAT: SPORTS

The sentences below all describe games and sports. Try to guess what the answer is from the descriptions.

1. In this game, two players or two pairs of players use rackets to hit a ball across a net.

2. This is a team game where the players kick a ball across a pitch, aiming to land it in the opposing team's goal.

3. This can be played on a field or an ice rink. Two teams of eleven players use long clubs to hit a puck or ball.

4. This is an outdoor game where the players will use bats, balls and wickets.

5. This is a game played on a court, where two teams of five players score by shooting a ball into a net.

6. This game involves batters and fielders. The person batting will attempt to run as far as possible around a diamond-shaped pitch.

7. This is a sport of attack and defence using a weapon called a foil and special protective clothing.

8. This martial art originated in Japan. It is a form of self-defence using blows and kicks and famous chopping movements of the hands.

9. Played on a course, the object of this game is to hit a small ball into a series of nine or 18 holes using a long club.

10. Also called table tennis, this game is played indoors on a table with small bats and a light, hollow ball.

11. In this team game, each player has a long stick with a netted pocket that is used for catching, carrying and throwing a small ball.

12. In this sport, people move a boat across water using oars.

13. In this sport, long, narrow runners are attached to the feet to glide down a slope, with the use of hand-held poles.

14. This sport is a race through water, using your arms and legs to propel yourself forward.

15. This is the sport of shooting at a target using a bow and arrow.

# GUESS THE REST: AROUND THE WORLD

The answer is given to each question below, but some of the letters are missing. Guess the rest of the letters correctly to make each answer complete.

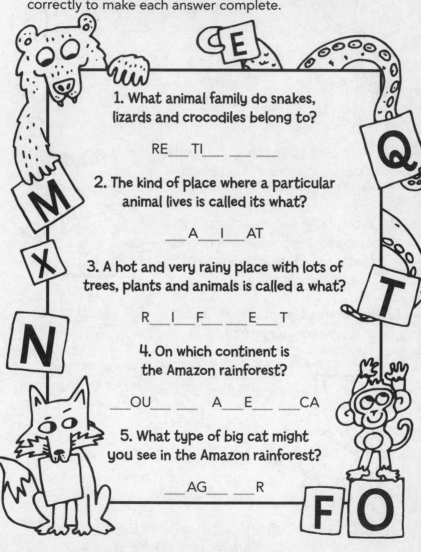

1. What animal family do snakes, lizards and crocodiles belong to?

RE___ TI___ ___ ___

2. The kind of place where a particular animal lives is called its what?

___ A ___ I ___ AT

3. A hot and very rainy place with lots of trees, plants and animals is called a what?

R ___ I ___ F ___ ___ E ___ T

4. On which continent is the Amazon rainforest?

___ OU ___ ___ A ___ E ___ ___ CA

5. What type of big cat might you see in the Amazon rainforest?

___ AG ___ ___ R

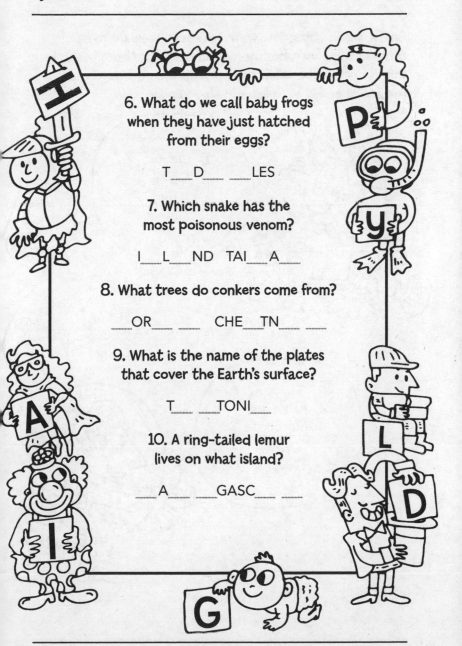

6. What do we call baby frogs when they have just hatched from their eggs?

T__D___ ___LES

7. Which snake has the most poisonous venom?

I__L__ND TAI__A__

8. What trees do conkers come from?

___OR___ ___ CHE__TN___ __

9. What is the name of the plates that cover the Earth's surface?

T__ ___TONI__

10. A ring-tailed lemur lives on what island?

__A__ ___GASC___ __

## ODD ONE OUT: COUNTRIES

Below are five lists. The words in each list relate to each other in some way, but there is an odd word out in each list that is not like the other three. Write the odd word out in the space below each list and also explain why.

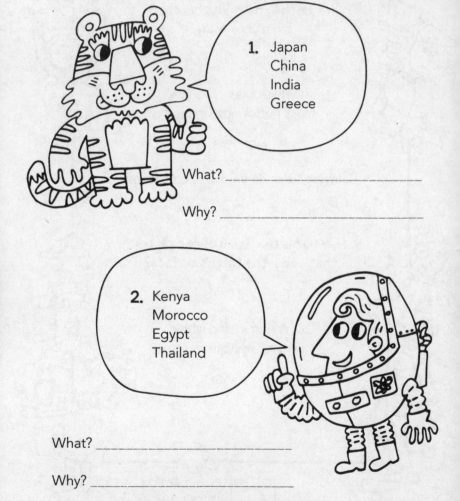

1. Japan
   China
   India
   Greece

What? _____

Why? _____

2. Kenya
   Morocco
   Egypt
   Thailand

What? _____

Why? _____

# Quiz 55

**3.** Germany
Italy
Poland
Peru

What? _____

Why? _____

**4.** Argentina
Bolivia
Venezuela
Norway

What? _____

Why? _____

**5.** Finland
India
Russia
Australia

What? _____

Why? _____

## HALL OF FAME: MUSIC

The multiple-choice questions below are all things that deserve a place in a hall of fame. Test your knowledge on the world's biggest, brightest and best.

1. **What is the Fender company famous for making?**
   a. Violins
   b. Saxophones
   c. Guitars

2. **What is the oldest known musical instrument?**
   a. Flute
   b. Guitar
   c. Harp

3. **How many strings does an acoustic guitar usually have?**
   a. 6
   b. 8
   c. 11

4. **Which tiny insect hollows out the wooden branches that are used to make didgeridoos?**
   a. Leafcutter ant
   b. Earwig
   c. Termite

5. **How long is the longest string on a standard harp?**
   a. 90 centimetres
   b. 152 centimetres
   c. 206 centimetres

6. **Which string instrument has the widest range of notes?**
   a. Cello
   b. Violin
   c. Viola

7. **Which of these instruments has only one string?**
   a. Fiddle
   b. Double bass
   c. Ektara

8. **An organ in the Atlantic City Convention Hall, USA, has an incredible number of pipes. How many does it have?**
   a. 10,220
   b. 33,112
   c. 8,111

9. **The instrument we call a piano is properly called a pianoforte. What does this mean in Italian?**
   a. Strong piano
   b. Flat and strong
   c. Soft and loud

10. **Which of these instruments is played with the mouth?**
    a. Harmonica
    b. Harmonium
    c. Accordion

## GUESS THE REST: SPACE

The answer is given to each question below, but some of the letters are missing. Guess the rest of the letters correctly to make each answer complete.

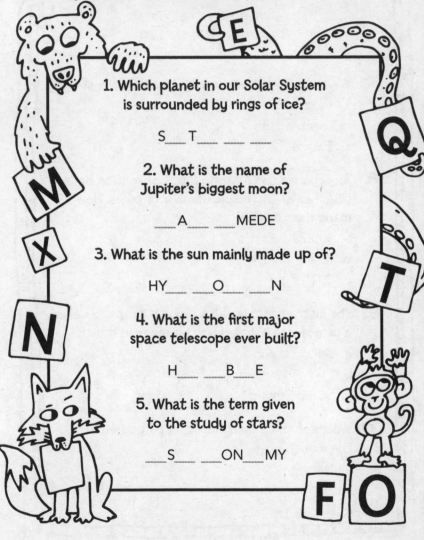

1. Which planet in our Solar System is surrounded by rings of ice?

S__ T___ ___ ___

2. What is the name of Jupiter's biggest moon?

___ A___ ___ MEDE

3. What is the sun mainly made up of?

HY___ ___O___ ___N

4. What is the first major space telescope ever built?

H___ ___ B___E

5. What is the term given to the study of stars?

___S___ ___ON___MY

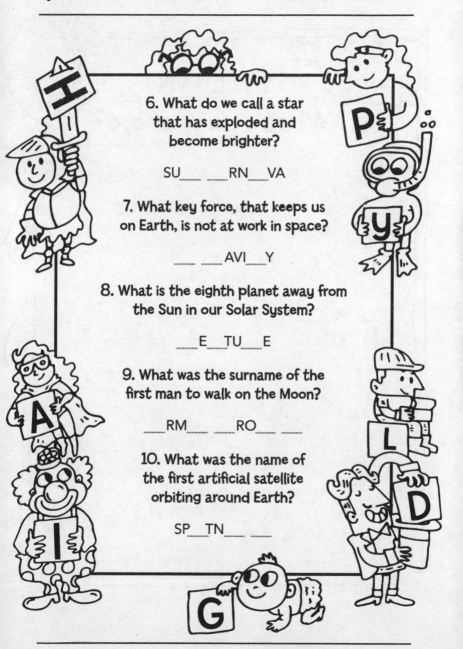

6. What do we call a star that has exploded and become brighter?

SU___ ___RN___VA

7. What key force, that keeps us on Earth, is not at work in space?

___ ___AVI___Y

8. What is the eighth planet away from the Sun in our Solar System?

___E___TU___E

9. What was the surname of the first man to walk on the Moon?

___RM___ ___RO___ ___

10. What was the name of the first artificial satellite orbiting around Earth?

SP___TN___ ___

# LEVEL TWO:
## What's your score?

Quiz 26 ..........       Quiz 43 ..........

Quiz 27 ..........       Quiz 44 ..........

Quiz 28 ..........       Quiz 45 ..........

Quiz 29 ..........       Quiz 46 ..........

Quiz 30 ..........       Quiz 47 ..........

Quiz 31 ..........       Quiz 48 ..........

Quiz 32 ..........       Quiz 49 ..........

Quiz 33 ..........       Quiz 50 ..........

Quiz 34 ..........       Quiz 51 ..........

Quiz 35 ..........       Quiz 52 ..........

Quiz 36 ..........       Quiz 53 ..........

Quiz 37 ..........       Quiz 54 ..........

Quiz 38 ..........       Quiz 55 ..........

Quiz 39 ..........       Quiz 56 ..........

Quiz 40 ..........       Quiz 57 ..........

Quiz 41 ..........

Quiz 42 ..........       Grand total ..............

LEVEL
THREE

## QUIZ SHOW: INVENTIONS

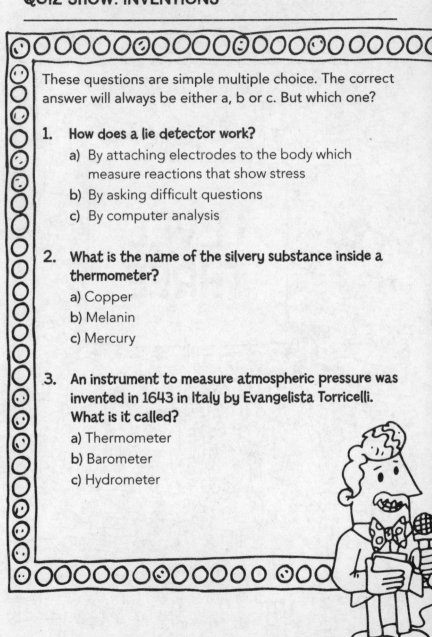

These questions are simple multiple choice. The correct answer will always be either a, b or c. But which one?

1.  **How does a lie detector work?**
    a) By attaching electrodes to the body which measure reactions that show stress
    b) By asking difficult questions
    c) By computer analysis

2.  **What is the name of the silvery substance inside a thermometer?**
    a) Copper
    b) Melanin
    c) Mercury

3.  **An instrument to measure atmospheric pressure was invented in 1643 in Italy by Evangelista Torricelli. What is it called?**
    a) Thermometer
    b) Barometer
    c) Hydrometer

4. **What is an abacus?**
   a) Musical instrument
   b) Printing press
   c) Counting instrument

5. **What is the name of the theory that the Universe originated with a huge explosion?**
   a) Big Bang theory
   b) Laws of motion
   c) Big Blast theory

6. **Which of these was invented by Benjamin Franklin?**
   a) The compass
   b) Bifocals
   c) Bunsen burner

7. **Who invented the electric light bulb in the USA in 1879?**
   a) Thomas Alva Edison
   b) Michael Faraday
   c) Lionel de Rothschild

# MISSING WORDS: MATHS

The sentences below each have a word missing. Pick the correct word from the box next to each sentence and write it in the space.

**1.** An _____ triangle is a triangle with two sides of equal length.

| Equilateral |
| Isosceles |
| Obtuse |

| Acute |
| Obtuse |
| Algorithm |

**2.** An angle less than 90 degrees is called an _____ angle.

**3.** There are _____ degrees in a right angle.

| 45 |
| 90 |
| 100 |

| Pentagon |
| Heptagon |
| Hexagon |

**4.** A _____ has five sides.

**5.** Geometry is the mathematics of

lines, angles and _____.

Shapes
Fractions
Percentages

Third dynamics
Divisible by three
Three dimensional

**6.** 3D stands for

_____.

**7.** Circumference is the length of the

outside of a _____.

Circle
Square
Diamond

Percentage
Ratio
Multiple

**8.** A _____ is a number

stated as a proportion of 100.

# TRUE OR FALSE: INVENTIONS

Are the statements below true or false? Tick the box you think is correct.

### 1. Archimedes invented the wheel.

☐ 👍 True or false? 👎 ☐

### 2. In 1876, Alexander Graham Bell invented Morse code.

☐ 👍 True or false? 👎 ☐

### 3. In 1885, the first aircraft was built in Germany, in a factory owned by Karl Benz.

☐ 👍 True or false? 👎 ☐

### 4. The television was invented by John Logie Baird.

☐ 👍 True or false? 👎 ☐

### 5. The soft drink Pepsi was invented in 1886 by John Pemberton.

☐ 👍 True or false? 👎 ☐

### 6. Clarence Birdseye invented the frozen food process in 1924.

☐ 👍 True or false? 👎 ☐

### 7. Charles Darwin invented the first traditional crossword puzzle in New York in 1913.

☐ 👍 True or false? 👎 ☐

**8. Plato invented the bathtub.**

☐ 👍 True or false? 👎 ☐

**9. The first hot air balloon to successfully carry people was invented in France in 1783.**

☐ 👍 True or false? 👎 ☐

**10. Dynamite was patented in Sweden in 1866.**

☐ 👍 True or false? 👎 ☐

**11. William Shakespeare invented the first newspaper.**

☐ 👍 True or false? 👎 ☐

**12. The microchip was invented in 1958.**

☐ 👍 True or false? 👎 ☐

**13. The Barbie doll was invented by a woman called Barbara Harry.**

☐ 👍 True or false? 👎 ☐

**14. The electric lamp was invented by Galileo.**

☐ 👍 True or false? 👎 ☐

**15. The first windmill was invented in ancient Persia.**

☐ 👍 True or false? 👎 ☐

# OUT OF ORDER: COUNTRIES

The words in the lists below are all in the wrong order.
Read the instructions above each list and then place the
words in the correct order by rewriting them in the spaces
on the right.

## 1. Place these continents by size, largest first.

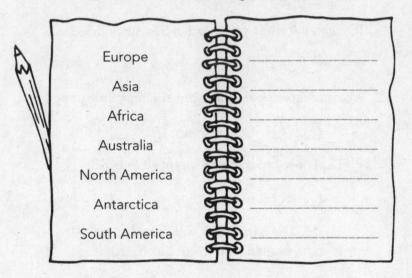

Europe

Asia

Africa

Australia

North America

Antarctica

South America

_____

_____

_____

_____

_____

_____

_____

# Quiz 61

## 2. Place these countries by population, largest first.

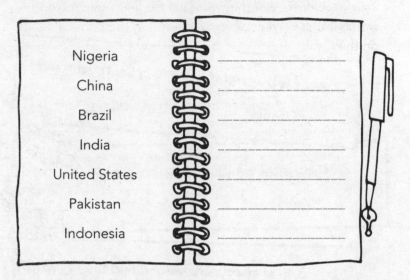

Nigeria

China

Brazil

India

United States

Pakistan

Indonesia

## 3. Place these countries by location, from North to South.

Poland

Greenland

Turkey

Norway

Argentina

Romania

Egypt

# WORD JUMBLE: COUNTRIES

The answers are given to all these questions below. The only problem is that they're all jumbled up. Unjumble the letters to reveal the correct answer.

**1. What is the largest country in South America?**

RABLIZ _____

**2. Beijing is the capital of which country?**

NICAH _____

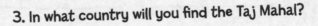

**3. In what country will you find the Taj Mahal?**

DINIA _____

**4. Which country has a blue flag with a red cross outlined in white?**

DILANEC _____

**5. Which country in the Pacific Ocean is made up of over 800 islands?**

JIIF _____

6. On what island are visitors greeted with a lei?

WAIHAI
_____

7. In which country is the city of St. Petersburg?

SIASUR
_____

8. Where does bratwurst come from?

NERGYAM
_____

9. What is the area around the South Pole called?

RATINCCATA
_____

10. What is the world's northernmost capital city?

KEYVIJKRA
_____

## HALL OF FAME: SPACE

The multiple-choice questions below are all things that deserve a place in a hall of fame. Test your knowledge on the world's biggest, brightest and best.

1.  **Which is the largest planet in our Solar System?**
    a. Jupiter
    b. Neptune
    c. Saturn

2.  **What is the largest moon in our Solar System?**
    a. Callisto
    b. Ganymede
    c. Europa

3.  **There are four rocky planets in our Solar System, which is the largest?**
    a. Earth
    b. Mercury
    c. Mars

4.  **What is the biggest object in our Solar System?**
    a. Jupiter
    b. Ganymede
    c. The Sun

5.  **Astronaut Valeri Polyakov holds the record for the longest human spaceflight in history. What is his record?**
    a. 237.4 days
    b. 437.7 days
    c. 507.2 days

6. Jerry L. Ross and Franklin Chang-Diaz share the record for the most spaceflights by humans. How many spaceflights have they achieved?
   a. 6
   b. 8
   c. 7

7. The oldest person to ever fly in space is American astronaut John Glen. How old was he?
   a. 67
   b. 77
   c. 85

8. Which planet is the smallest?
   a. Mercury
   b. Neptune
   c. Earth

9. Which planet in our Solar System has the most moons?
   a. Neptune
   b. Jupiter
   c. Saturn

10. What was the first mammal to go into space?
    a. Dog
    b. Rhesus monkey
    c. Siamese cat

## MATCH UP: GEOGRAPHY

Below are three sets of lists. Each word in the left-hand list can be matched up with a word in the right. Match all the words until they are all paired up.

### Match up the country with its capital city.

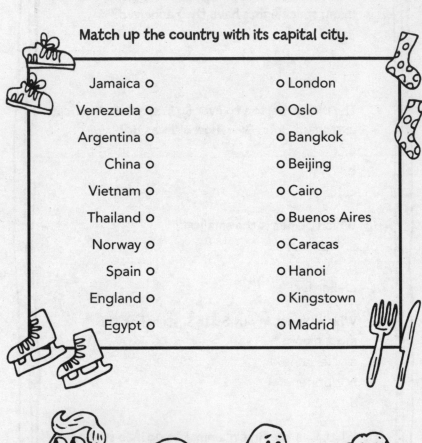

| | |
|---|---|
| Jamaica o | o London |
| Venezuela o | o Oslo |
| Argentina o | o Bangkok |
| China o | o Beijing |
| Vietnam o | o Cairo |
| Thailand o | o Buenos Aires |
| Norway o | o Caracas |
| Spain o | o Hanoi |
| England o | o Kingstown |
| Egypt o | o Madrid |

# Quiz 64

Score................................

## Match up the city with its continent.

| | |
|---|---|
| Casablanca o | o Europe |
| Sydney o | o Asia |
| Caracas o | o North America |
| Chicago o | o South America |
| Tokyo o | o Australia |
| Rome o | o Africa |

## Match up the country with its national dish.

| | |
|---|---|
| Pakistan o | o Moules-frites |
| Turkey o | o Peking duck |
| Ireland o | o Bratwurst |
| Germany o | o Colcannon |
| Spain o | o Biryani |
| Russia o | o Pierogi |
| Poland o | o Borscht |
| Belgium o | o Paella |
| China o | o Kebab |

# GUESS WHAT: SPACE

The sentences below all describe things relating to space. Try to guess what the answer is from the descriptions.

1. This is the largest planet. It is a gas planet that is stripy in appearance and has a large red spot on its surface.

2. This was once the smallest planet in the Solar System, but in 2006 it was considered too small to be a planet and is now called a dwarf planet.

3. This is a planet that is famous for its rings. It is the sixth planet from the Sun.

4. This is the centre of our Solar System and is the hottest object in it.

5. This is the only planet known to support life. It is the planet humans call home.

6. These are small objects in space consisting of frozen gas, dust and rock. They have trailing tails. They follow an orbit around the Sun.

7. There are thousands of these rocky objects orbiting the Sun, mainly in a group called a belt between Mars and Jupiter.

8. These regions of space form when a large star collapses in on itself. Their gravitational pull is so strong that not even light can escape.

9. This is Earth's natural satellite. You can see it in the night sky and it influences the tides.

10. These twinkle in the night sky and look very small, but are actually just very far away. Our own Sun is one of these.

11. This is the layer of gas that surrounds a planet, especially the Earth, and is held to it by gravity.

12. This is a small planet that is fourth closest to the Sun. It is known as 'the red planet'.

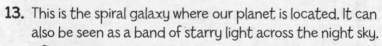

13. This is the spiral galaxy where our planet is located. It can also be seen as a band of starry light across the night sky.

14. This is an arrangement consisting of a central star and the celestial bodies that orbit it.

15. This is a huge collection of stars, dust and gas, held together by gravity. There are billions of these in the Universe.

## GUESS THE REST: SEAS AND OCEANS

The answer is given to each question below, but some of the letters are missing. Guess the rest of the letters correctly to make each answer complete.

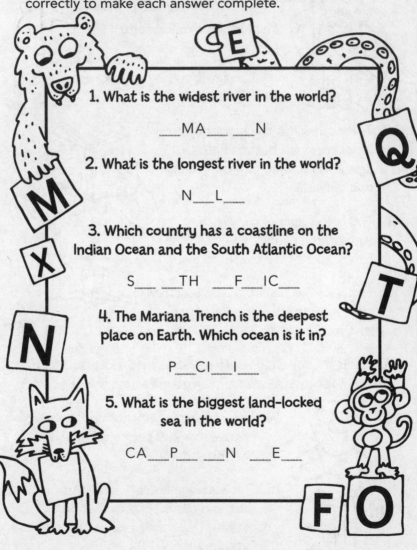

1. What is the widest river in the world?

___MA___ ___N

2. What is the longest river in the world?

N___L___

3. Which country has a coastline on the Indian Ocean and the South Atlantic Ocean?

S___ ___TH ___F___IC___

4. The Mariana Trench is the deepest place on Earth. Which ocean is it in?

P___CI___I___

5. What is the biggest land-locked sea in the world?

CA___P___ ___N ___E___

6. Which Mediterranean city
is spread over 118 islands?

\_\_ E \_ IC \_\_

7. The Hudson River flows
through which city?

N\_\_ W \_\_ \_\_ \_\_ \_\_K

8. Dubai is a city on the coast of which sea?

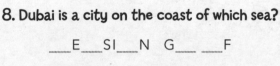

\_\_ E \_ SI\_ N G\_\_ \_\_F

9. Which ocean is almost completely
covered by sea ice in the winter?

\_\_ R\_\_ TI\_\_

10. What is the name of
the river that flows
through Amsterdam?

A\_ S\_\_ \_\_ L

# ODD ONE OUT: SPORTS TEAMS

Below are five lists. The words in each list relate to each other in some way, but there is an odd word out in each list that is not like the other three. Write the odd word out in the space below each list and also explain why.

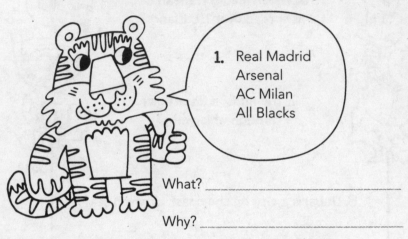

1. Real Madrid
   Arsenal
   AC Milan
   All Blacks

What? _____

Why? _____

2. Manchester United
   Bayern Munich
   Paris Saint-Germain
   Chicago White Socks

What? _____

Why? _____

**3.** Boston Red Socks
New York Yankees
Atlanta Braves
Manchester City

What? _____

Why? _____

**4.** Golden State Warriors
Chicago Bulls
New York Knicks
New Jersey Devils

What? _____

Why? _____

**5.** Detroit Red Wings
Vancouver Canucks
Chicago Blackhawks
Leeds Rhinos

What? _____

Why? _____

## QUIZ SHOW: SPACE

These questions are simple multiple choice. The correct answer will always be either a, b or c. But which one?

1.  **What is the largest planet in our Solar System?**
    a) Mars
    b) Neptune
    c) Jupiter

2.  **What is the name of the comet that visits our inner Solar System every 76 years?**
    a) Donati's
    b) Halley's
    c) Beila's

3.  **The distance of stars from the Earth is measured in which units?**
    a) Light-years
    b) Light-bytes
    c) Solar years

4.  **What is a corona?**
    a) A halo of light around the Sun
    b) Planetary rings, as around Saturn
    c) The path of a moon around its planet

5. **What is the name given to the path of a planet around the Sun?**
   a) The solar path
   b) Its orbit
   c) The zodiac

6. **Which planet has a total of 16 moons, including Europa, Ganymede, Leda, and Thebe?**
   a) Jupiter
   b) Venus
   c) Saturn

7. **Where are the Sea of Serenity, the Bay of Rainbows, the Sea of Clouds and the Lake of Dreams?**
   a) On Mars
   b) On the Sun
   c) On the Moon

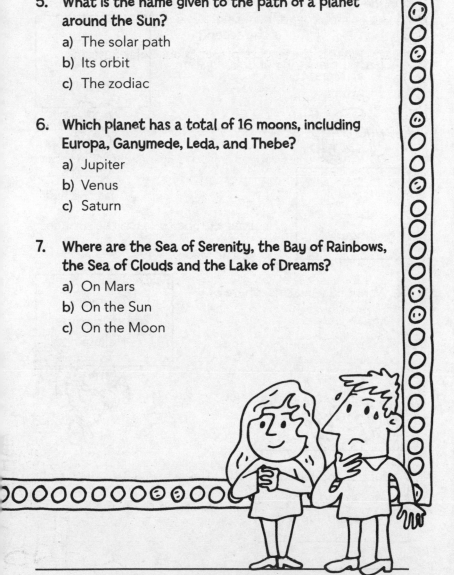

# MISSING WORDS: SPACE

The sentences below each have a word missing. Pick the correct word from the box next to each sentence and write it in the space.

1. _____ is the second

largest planet in our Solar System.

Neptune
Saturn
Mercury

Luna 2
Apollo 2
Ranger 1

2. _____ was the first

space probe to reach the surface

of the Moon.

3. Venus has an atmosphere of

mainly _____.

Oxygen
Carbon dioxide
Helium

Jupiter and Saturn
Earth and Mars
Mars and Jupiter

4. The Asteroid Belt is located

between the planets

_____.

## Quiz 69

**5.** The study of celestial objects is called _____.

Astronomy
Astrology
Solar observation

Dwarf planet
Asteroid
Moon

**6.** In 2006, Pluto was reclassified as a _____.

**7.** The planet _____ has a giant red spot much wider than the Earth.

Mars
Saturn
Jupiter

Mars
Mercury
Neptune

**8.** _____ is the planet nearest to the Sun.

# TRUE OR FALSE: MYTHS AND LEGENDS

Are the statements below true or false? Tick the box you think is correct.

### 1. A dryad is a woodland nymph.

☐ True or false? ☐

### 2. In Greek mythology, the Furies punish crimes.

☐ True or false? ☐

### 3. A garibaldi is a male fairy.

☐ True or false? ☐

### 4. A python is a mythical snake.

☐ True or false? ☐

### 5. Baosheng Dadi is the Chinese god of medicine.

☐ True or false? ☐

### 6. Icarus is the Greek goddess of love.

☐ True or false? ☐

### 7. A sprite is a mythical winged horse.

☐ True or false? ☐

### 8. Leprechauns are said to come from Ireland.

☐ True or false? ☐

9. In Greek mythology, Medusa is a hideous monster with rat tails for hair.

☐ 👍 True or false? 👎 ☐

10. A natterjack is a trick-playing elf.

☐ 👍 True or false? 👎 ☐

11. In Greek mythology, the Styx is a river you have to cross to get to the Underworld.

☐ 👍 True or false? 👎 ☐

12. In Hindu mythology there are 14 worlds – seven higher worlds and seven lower ones.

☐ 👍 True or false? 👎 ☐

13. Neptune was the Roman god of the sea.

☐ 👍 True or false? 👎 ☐

14. Olympus was the home of the Greek Gods

☐ 👍 True or false? 👎 ☐

15. In Japanese mythology, the first gods to come into existence were called Kotoamatsukami.

☐ 👍 True or false? 👎 ☐

# OUT OF ORDER: BIOLOGY

The words in the lists below are all in the wrong order. Read the instructions above each list and then place the words in the correct order by rewriting them in the spaces on the right.

## 1. Place these human bones by length, longest first.

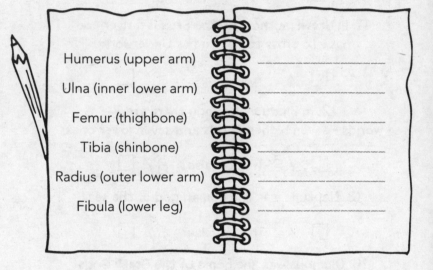

Humerus (upper arm) _____

Ulna (inner lower arm) _____

Femur (thighbone) _____

Tibia (shinbone) _____

Radius (outer lower arm) _____

Fibula (lower leg) _____

## 2. Place these human organs by weight, heaviest first.

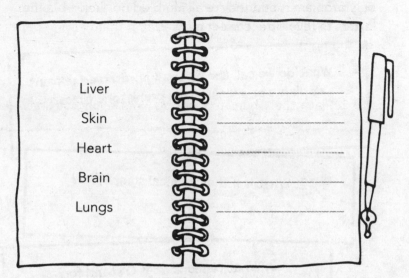

Liver

Skin

Heart

Brain

Lungs

## 3. Place these mammals by brain size, largest first.

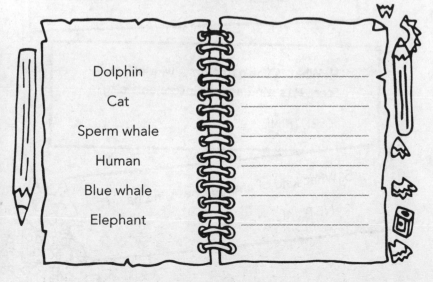

Dolphin

Cat

Sperm whale

Human

Blue whale

Elephant

# WORD JUMBLE: SCIENCE

The answers are given to all these questions below. The only problem is that they're all jumbled up. Unjumble the letters to reveal the correct answer.

1. What do we call the naturally preserved remains of plants or animals from prehistoric times?

SOFILSS _____

2. What is H the chemical symbol for?

NEGDYROH _____

3. What element does O stand for?

YOXEGN _____

4. What is the name for a windmill that converts wind energy into electricity?

BUTRINE _____

5. What kind of energy does wind have?

NETCIKI _____

6. What is it called when atoms join together to release energy?

UNIOSF

_____

7. What can a meteorite create in the ground when it lands?

TARCER

_____

8. What organ in the body is most like a camera?

YEE

_____

9. What is the Earth's largest natural satellite?

MONO

_____

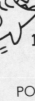

10. What instrument is used to look at distant objects?

POLEETSCE

_____

# HALL OF FAME: HISTORY

The multiple-choice questions below are all things that deserve a place in a hall of fame. Test your knowledge on the world's biggest, brightest and best.

1. **Who was the only wife of Henry VIII to survive him?**
   a. Anne Boleyn
   b. Catherine of Aragon
   c. Catherine Parr

2. **Which African American woman famously refused to give up her seat on a bus?**
   a. Rosa Parks
   b. Joan of Ark
   c. Hilary Clinton

3. **What was the name of the first President of the USA?**
   a. George Washington
   b. George Bush
   c. Barack Obama

4. **At what famous battle did Wellington defeat Napoleon?**
   a. Somme
   b. Waterloo
   c. Balaklava

5. **Which European explorer first reached North America?**
   a. Leif Erikson
   b. Christopher Columbus
   c. Robert Falcon Scott

6. **Who famously tried to blow up the British Parliament in The Gunpowder Plot?**
   a. Samuel Pepys
   b. Guy Fawkes
   c. Thomas Paine

7. **How many cities is Alexander the Great said to have founded?**
   a. 25
   b. 120
   c. 70

8. **What gory revolution became known as the Reign of Terror?**
   a. Russian Revolution
   b. French Revolution
   c. American Civil War

9. **What was the deadliest battle in the American Civil War?**
   a. Battle of Gettysburg
   b. Battle of the Wilderness
   c. Battle of Chickmauga

10. **Who was the only person allowed to wear a fully purple toga in the Roman Empire?**
    a. The Emperor
    b. The Governor
    c. The Chief Magistrate

# MATCH UP: MUSICAL INSTRUMENTS

Below are three sets of lists. Each word in the left-hand list can be matched up with a word in the right. Match all the words until they are all paired up.

## Match up the features with the musical instrument.

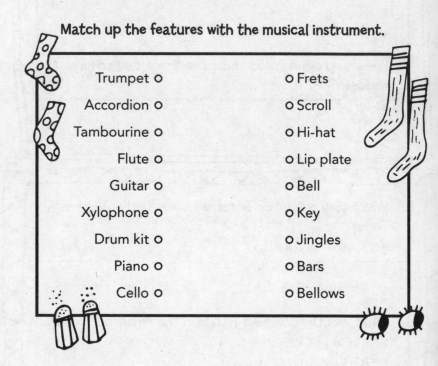

| | |
|---|---|
| Trumpet o | o Frets |
| Accordion o | o Scroll |
| Tambourine o | o Hi-hat |
| Flute o | o Lip plate |
| Guitar o | o Bell |
| Xylophone o | o Key |
| Drum kit o | o Jingles |
| Piano o | o Bars |
| Cello o | o Bellows |

## Quiz 74

Score.............................

Match up these instruments with their orchestra section.

Viola o      o Woodwind

Timpani o      o Brass

Flute o      o String

Cornet o      o Percussion

Match up the musical instrument
with another in the same group.

Trombone o      o Viola

Cello o      o Tuba

Flute o      o Tambourine

Drums o      o Clarinet

## GUESS WHAT: COUNTRIES AND CITIES

The sentences below all describe cities or countries. Try to guess what the answer is from the descriptions.

1. This is the capital city of Argentina. Its name means 'good airs'.

2. This European city is home to the Eiffel Tower and the Louvre.

3. This is a very sacred place. Every year millions of Muslims travel here on a pilgrimage called the Hajj.

4. This is the biggest city in Australia but it is not the capital.

5. This is a very old Italian city and has many ruins, including the Forum and the Colosseum.

6. This is the capital of Bolivia and the highest capital city above sea level in the world.

7. This city spreads across 118 little islands that are all separated by canals. Some people use a gondola to get around.

8. This is a city with an enormously tall building in it: the Burj Khalifa.

9. This country is the source of whisky, linen and mythical creatures called leprechauns.

10. This is a separate country found in the middle of Rome. It is home to the Pope.

11. This European country is bordered by France and Poland. It is home to the Berlin Wall.

12. This is a European country that some people think is shaped like a boot. It has many beautiful cities, including Florence and Milan.

13. This is the longest and the thinnest country in South America. Its capital is Santiago.

14. This is a Chinese region known for its extensive skyline and harbour. It is one of the most populated areas in the world.

15. This is the most densely populated city in India. It lies on the west coast.

# GUESS THE REST: MYTHOLOGY

The answer is given to each question below, but some of the letters are missing. Guess the rest of the letters correctly to make each answer complete.

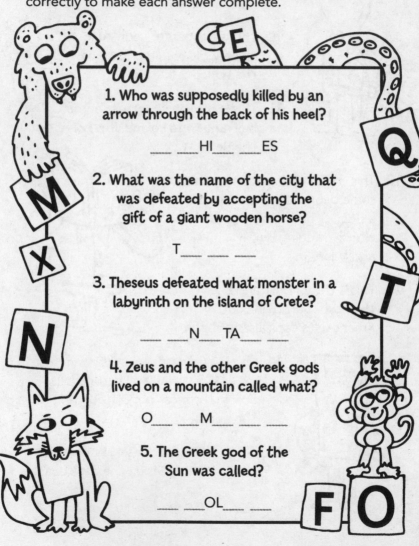

1. Who was supposedly killed by an arrow through the back of his heel?

___ ___ HI ___ ___ ES

2. What was the name of the city that was defeated by accepting the gift of a giant wooden horse?

T___ ___ ___

3. Theseus defeated what monster in a labyrinth on the island of Crete?

___ ___ N ___ TA ___ ___ ___

4. Zeus and the other Greek gods lived on a mountain called what?

O ___ ___ M ___ ___ ___ ___

5. The Greek god of the Sun was called?

___ ___ OL ___ ___ ___

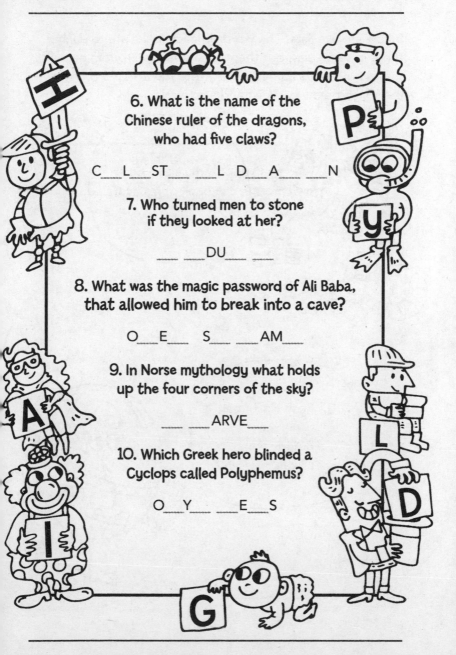

6. What is the name of the Chinese ruler of the dragons, who had five claws?

C _ _ L _ ST _ _ _ L D _ A _ _ N

7. Who turned men to stone if they looked at her?

_ _ _ _ _ _ DU _ _ _ _

8. What was the magic password of Ali Baba, that allowed him to break into a cave?

O _ E _ S _ _ AM _ _

9. In Norse mythology what holds up the four corners of the sky?

_ _ _ _ _ ARVE _ _ _

10. Which Greek hero blinded a Cyclops called Polyphemus?

O _ Y _ _ E _ S

## ODD ONE OUT: CULTURE

Below are five lists. The words in each list relate to each other in some way, but there is an odd word out in each list that is not like the other three. Write the odd word out in the space below each list and also explain why.

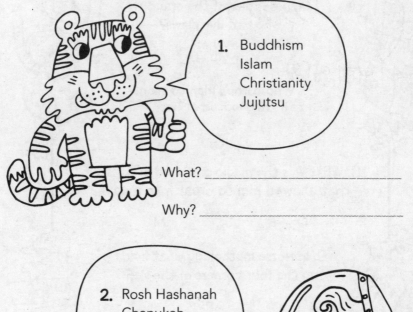

1.  Buddhism
    Islam
    Christianity
    Jujutsu

What? _____

Why? _____

2.  Rosh Hashanah
    Chanukah
    Bat Mitzvah
    Diwali

What? _____

Why? _____

3. Mosque
Cathedral
Synagogue
Castle

What? _____

Why? _____

4. Lantern Festival
Dragon Boat Festival
Spring Festival
Holly Festival

What? _____

Why? _____

5. Shiva
Vishnu
Brahma
Izanagi

What? _____

Why? _____

# OUT OF ORDER: GEOGRAPHY

The words in the lists below are all in the wrong order. Read the instructions above each list and then place the words in the correct order by rewriting them in the spaces on the right.

**1. Place these American states by population, largest first.**

Vermont

Tennessee

California

Rhode Island

Ohio

Kansas

**2. Place these countries by length
of coastline, longest first.**

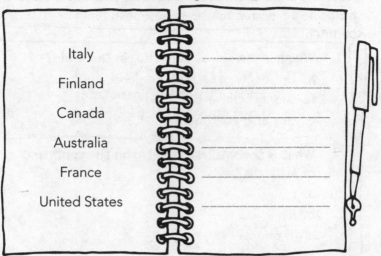

Italy

Finland

Canada

Australia

France

United States

**3. Place these countries by size, largest first.**

Spain

Japan

Russia

Australia

Egypt

# HALL OF FAME: WORLD KNOWLEDGE

The multiple-choice questions below are all things that deserve a place in a hall of fame. Test your knowledge on the world's biggest, brightest and best.

1. **Which is the oldest university in the world?**
   a. University of Oxford, England
   b. Istanbul University, Turkey
   c. University of Karueein, Morocco

2. **What is the smallest country on the continent of Australia?**
   a. Nauru
   b. Fiji
   c. Tasmania

3. **What is the oldest castle to have been continuously lived in?**
   a. Chateau Gaillard, France
   b. Himeji castle, Japan
   c. Windsor castle, UK

4. **Which is the only continent not to have a desert?**
   a. Australia
   b. Europe
   c. Antarctica

5. **Which is the oldest religion?**
   a. Hinduism
   b. Mormonism
   c. Catholicism

6.  **How many European countries still have a monarchy?**
    a. 10
    b. 6
    c. 18

7.  **Which country has the oldest monarchy?**
    a. Russia
    b. Japan
    c. England

8.  **Who was the first woman to be Prime Minister of Britain?**
    a. Margaret Thatcher
    b. Lady Diana
    c. Princess Margaret

9.  **What is the likely number of people who lived in the Roman Empire at its peak?**
    a. 60 million
    b. 10 million
    c. 90 million

10. **Which continent contains the most countries?**
    a. South America
    b. Australia
    c. Africa

## MATCH UP: HISTORY

Below are three sets of lists. Each word in the left-hand list can be matched up with a word in the right. Match all the words until they are all paired up.

### Match up these historical eras with their countries.

| | |
|---|---|
| Gilded Age o | o China |
| Victorian Era o | o Italy |
| Kamakura period o | o Turkey |
| Mughal Empire o | o India |
| Ottoman Empire o | o Japan |
| Ming dynasty o | o USA |
| Renaissance o | o UK |

### Match up these modern and historical rulers or heads of state with their countries.

| | |
|---|---|
| King Constantine II o | o England |
| Louis XVI o | o USA |
| Emperor Qianlong o | o Germany |
| Tony Abbott o | o China |
| Abraham Lincoln o | o France |
| Queen Elizabeth I o | o Greece |
| Kaiser Wilhelm o | o Australia |

**Match up these historical landmarks with their country.**

| | |
|---|---|
| Mount Rushmore o | o France |
| Machu Piccu o | o Italy |
| Saint Basil's Cathedral o | o England |
| Brandenburg Gate o | o India |
| The Little Mermaid o | o Egypt |
| The Great Sphinx o | o Denmark |
| Tower of Pisa o | o Peru |
| Taj Mahal o | o Germany |
| Eiffel Tower o | o USA |
| Big Ben o | o Russia |

# LEVEL THREE:
## What's your score?

ALL THE
ANSWERS

# ALL THE ANSWERS

## LEVEL ONE

### QUIZ 1: QUIZ SHOW: POLAR REGIONS
**1.** b    **3.** a    **5.** b    **7.** b
**2.** c    **4.** c    **6.** b

### QUIZ 2: MISSING WORDS: ANIMALS
**1.** Horse    **3.** Drone    **5.** Eight    **7.** Antarctic
**2.** Deer    **4.** Camel    **6.** Fox    **8.** Badger

### QUIZ 3: TRUE OR FALSE: INSECTS
**1.** True    **5.** False    **9.** False    **13.** False
**2.** False    **6.** False    **10.** True    **14.** True
**3.** True    **7.** True    **11.** False    **15.** True
**4.** True    **8.** False    **12.** False

### QUIZ 4: OUT OF ORDER: ANIMALS
**1.** Blue whale, Asian elephant, Rhinoceros, Saltwater crocodile, King penguin

**2.** Cheetah, Greyhound, Elephant, Tortoise, Snail

**3.** Ostrich, King penguin, Bald eagle, Pigeon, Robin

### QUIZ 5: WORD JUMBLE: ANIMALS
**1.** Rabbit    **6.** Hippopotamus
**2.** Dalmatian    **7.** Pelican
**3.** Orangutan    **8.** Lion
**4.** Honey bee    **9.** Dinosaur
**5.** African elephant    **10.** Amphibian

### QUIZ 6: HALL OF FAME: ANIMALS
**1.** a    **4.** c    **7.** b    **10.** b
**2.** c    **5.** a    **8.** b
**3.** b    **6.** c    **9.** a

## QUIZ 7: MATCH UP: COLOURS

1. Red – Ruby
   Blue – Sapphire
   Green – Emerald
   White – Diamond
   Orange – Amber
   Purple – Amethyst

2. Red – Strawberry
   Purple – Grapes

   Yellow – Banana
   Orange – Satsuma
   Blue – Blueberry

3. Yellow – Sunflower
   Purple – Violet
   Red – Poppy
   Blue – Cornflower
   Pink – Cherry blossom

## QUIZ 8: GUESS WHAT: ANIMALS

1. Giraffe
2. Sloth
3. Parrot
4. Kangaroo
5. Ant
6. Hyena
7. Owl
8. Snake
9. Fox
10. Woodpecker
11. Blue whale
12. Dog
13. Lion
14. Octopus
15. Crab

## QUIZ 9: GUESS THE REST: SCIENCE

1. Sixty
2. Rocket
3. Metal
4. Candle
5. Star
6. Electricity
7. Carbon dioxide
8. Vibrations
9. Milk
10. Graphite

## QUIZ 10: ODD ONE OUT: CLOTHING

1. What?: Shorts
   Why?: Shorts are worn in hot weather, the other items are worn in cold weather.

2. What?: Pyjamas
   Why?: Pyjamas are worn to bed, the other items are worn when diving.

3. What?: Flip flops
   Why?: Flip flops are worn in hot weather, the other items are worn skiing.

# ALL THE ANSWERS

4. What?: Skirt
   Why?: Skirts are not worn when swimming, the other items are.

5. What?: Slippers
   Why?: Slippers are worn indoors, the other items are worn outdoors.

## QUIZ 11: QUIZ SHOW: PREHISTORIC WORLD

| | | | |
|---|---|---|---|
| 1. a | 3. a | 5. a | 7. b |
| 2. b | 4. a | 6. b | |

## QUIZ 12: MISSING WORDS: PLANTS

| | | |
|---|---|---|
| 1. Oak | 4. Apples | 7. Deforestation |
| 2. Flowers | 5. Sap | 8. Evergreen |
| 3. Attract insects | 6. Deciduous | |

## QUIZ 13: TRUE OR FALSE: ANIMALS

| | | | |
|---|---|---|---|
| 1. False | 5. True | 9. False | 13. False |
| 2. False | 6. False | 10. False | 14. True |
| 3. False | 7. True | 11. False | 15. True |
| 4. True | 8. True | 12. True | |

## QUIZ 14: OUT OF ORDER: HISTORY

1. George Washington, Abraham Lincoln, John F. Kennedy, Bill Clinton, Barack Obama

2. King William I, King Henry VIII, Queen Elizabeth I, Queen Victoria, Queen Elizabeth II

3. Battle of Troy, Battle of Hastings, Battle of Waterloo, Battle of Gettysburg, Battle of the Somme

## QUIZ 15: WORD JUMBLE: SCHOOL SUBJECTS

1. Geography
2. History
3. Games
4. Drama
5. Spanish
6. French
7. Mathematics
8. Science
9. Art
10. Music

## QUIZ 16: MATCH UP: ANIMALS

1. Tiger – Cub
   Dog – Puppy
   Cat – Kitten
   Rabbit – Kit
   Deer – Fawn
   Cow – Calf
   Hen – Chick
   Fish – Fry
   Goose – Gosling

   Bee – Queen
   Chicken – Hen
   Pig – Sow
   Horse – Mare
   Sheep – Ewe
   Donkey – Jenny

2. Fox – Vixen
   Deer – Doe
   Goat – Nanny goat

3. Shark – Ocean
   Bird – Tree
   Cow – Field
   Frog – Pond
   Badger – Woodland
   Giraffe – Savannah

## QUIZ 17: GUESS WHAT: HUMAN BODY

1. Legs
2. Arms
3. Teeth
4. Eyes
5. Fingers
6. Heart
7. Brain
8. Skeleton
9. Ears
10. Nails
11. Knee
12. Feet
13. Hair
14. Nose
15. Skin

## QUIZ 18: GUESS THE REST: WHERE DO YOU GO?

1. Bathroom
2. Classroom
3. Supermarket
4. Garage
5. Library
6. Park
7. Railway station
8. Post office
9. Restaurant
10. Bakery

## ALL THE ANSWERS

### QUIZ 19: ODD ONE OUT: TRANSPORT

1. What?: Car
   Why?: All the others run on rails, a car does not.

2. What?: Tractor
   Why?: A tractor does not have two wheels, all the others do.

3. What?: Taxi
   Why?: A taxi does not travel by air, all the others do.

4. What?: Bus
   Why?: A bus is not a construction vehicle, all the others are.

5. What?: Coach
   Why?: A coach does not travel by water, all the others do.

### QUIZ 20: QUIZ SHOW: MYTHS AND LEGENDS

| | | | |
|---|---|---|---|
| 1. b | 3. b | 5. a | 7. a |
| 2. a | 4. c | 6. b | |

### QUIZ 21: MISSING WORDS: BIRDS

| | | | |
|---|---|---|---|
| 1. Talon | 3. Male | 5. Cygnet | 7. Africa |
| 2. Penguin | 4. Owls | 6. Albatross | 8. Feathers |

### QUIZ 22: TRUE OR FALSE: SPACE

| | | | |
|---|---|---|---|
| 1. True | 5. False | 9. True | 13. True |
| 2. False | 6. True | 10. False | 14. False |
| 3. False | 7. True | 11. True | 15. True |
| 4. False | 8. False | 12. True | |

### QUIZ 23: WORD JUMBLE: HOBBIES

| | |
|---|---|
| 1. Reading | 6. Cooking |
| 2. Movie | 7. Listening to music |
| 3. Cycling | 8. Dancing |
| 4. Drawing | 9. Horse riding |
| 5. Watching TV | 10. Sleepover |

## QUIZ 24: GUESS WHAT: EVERYDAY THINGS

1. Newspaper
2. Wellington boots
3. Umbrella
4. Lamp
5. Front door
6. Boat
7. Kettle
8. Television
9. Car
10. Flowers
11. Glue
12. Mobile phone
13. Magazine
14. Supermarket
15. Clock

## QUIZ 25: ODD ONE OUT: SCHOOL

1. What?: History
   Why?: History is not a language, the other subjects are.

2. What?: Eraser
   Why?: An eraser is not used to write with, all the others are.

3. What?: Pencil sharpener
   Why?: A pencil sharpener is not mathematical equipment, all the others are.

4. What?: Calculator
   Why?: A calculator is not used in art, all the others are.

5. What?: Pupils
   Why?: Pupils are not employed by a school, all the other people are.

LEVEL TWO

## QUIZ 26: QUIZ SHOW: HUMAN BODY

1. c
2. a
3. b
4. a
5. a
6. c
7. b

# ALL THE ANSWERS

## QUIZ 27: MISSING WORDS: TIME
1. 20:30
2. United Kingdom
3. 3 hours
4. 52
5. Sundial
6. Light-year
7. Horology
8. Nanosecond

## QUIZ 28: TRUE OR FALSE: NATURAL WORLD
1. True
2. False
3. False
4. True
5. False
6. True
7. True
8. False
9. False
10. True
11. False
12. True
13. False
14. False
15. True

## QUIZ 29: OUT OF ORDER: SPACE
1. Mercury, Venus, Earth, Mars, Jupiter, Saturn, Uranus, Neptune

2. New Moon, Waxing crescent, First quarter, Waxing gibbous, Full Moon, Waning gibbous, Third quarter, Waning crescent

3. Jupiter, Saturn, Neptune, Uranus, Earth, Mars, Mercury, Venus

## QUIZ 30: WORD JUMBLE: SPORTS
1. Baseball
2. Cricket
3. Rugby
4. Netball
5. Hockey
6. Ice skating
7. Gymnastics
8. Swimming
9. Beijing
10. Trampolining

## QUIZ 31: HALL OF FAME: GEOGRAPHY
1. a
2. a
3. c
4. b
5. b
6. c
7. a
8. b
9. c
10. a

### QUIZ 32: MATCH UP: COUNTRIES

1. Phoenix – Arizona
   Houston – Texas
   San Jose – California
   Jacksonville – Florida
   Memphis – Tennessee
   Milwaukee – Wisconsin
   Wichita – Kansas
   Cleveland – Ohio
   Charlotte – North Carolina

2. Yen – Japan
   Franc – Switzerland
   Krona – Sweden
   Ruble – Russia
   Dollar – Singapore
   Lira – Turkey
   Peso – Mexico
   Yuan – China
   Euro – France

3. Germany – Poland
   China – Mongolia
   Morocco – Algeria
   Norway – Sweden
   Argentina – Chile
   Colombia – Peru

### QUIZ 33: GUESS WHAT: OCCUPATIONS

1. Train driver
2. Police officer
3. Builder
4. Dancer
5. Actor
6. Writer
7. Banker
8. Artist
9. Teacher
10. Gardener
11. Singer
12. Zoo keeper
13. Waiter
14. Footballer
15. Pilot

### QUIZ 34: GUESS THE REST: ANIMALS

1. Tusks
2. Bamboo shoots
3. Raptors
4. Marsupials
5. Den
6. Herbivore
7. Chrysalis
8. Frogspawn
9. Emperor
10. Talons

### QUIZ 35: ODD ONE OUT: MUSICAL INSTRUMENTS

1. What?: French horn
   Why?: A French horn is not a percussion instrument, all the others are.

2. What?: Wooden
   Why?: Wooden is not an instrumental group, all the others are.

3.  What?: Cymbals
    Why?: Cymbals are not a string instrument, all the others are.

4.  What?: Bongo
    Why?: A bongo has not got strings, all the others do.

5.  What?: Tuba
    Why?: A tuba is a brass instrument, all the others are woodwind.

## QUIZ 36: QUIZ SHOW: NUMBERS

| | | | |
|---|---|---|---|
| **1.** b | **3.** c | **5.** a | **7.** c |
| **2.** b | **4.** a | **6.** c | |

## QUIZ 37: MISSING WORDS: COLOURS

| | | |
|---|---|---|
| **1.** Seven | **4.** Orange | **7.** Light |
| **2.** Green | **5.** Spectrum | **8.** Shorter than |
| **3.** Yellow | **6.** White | |

## QUIZ 38: TRUE OR FALSE: GEOGRAPHY

| | | | |
|---|---|---|---|
| **1.** True | **5.** True | **9.** False | **13.** True |
| **2.** False | **6.** False | **10.** False | **14.** False |
| **3.** True | **7.** True | **11.** False | **15.** True |
| **4.** True | **8.** True | **12.** True | |

## QUIZ 39: OUT OF ORDER: NUMBERS

**1.** I, II, III, IV, V, VI, VII, VIII

**2.** Byte, Kilobyte, Megabyte, Gigabyte, Terabyte

**3.** Pentagon, Hexagon, Heptagon, Octagon, Nonagon, Decagon, Hendecagon

## QUIZ 40: WORD JUMBLE: FOOTWEAR

1. Flip flops
2. Trainers
3. Cowboy boots
4. High heels
5. Wellington boots
6. Slippers
7. Flippers
8. Ballet shoes
9. Walking boots
10. Clogs

## QUIZ 41: HALL OF FAME: COUNTRIES

1. c
2. a
3. b
4. a
5. a
6. a
7. c
8. c
9. c
10. b

## QUIZ 42: MATCH UP: ANIMALS

1. Fur – Rabbit
   Talons – Eagle
   Scales – Fish
   Fangs – Snake
   Mane – Horse
   Bill – Duck
   Tusks – Elephant
   Snout – Pig
   Flippers – Penguin
   Hands – Chimpanzee

   Bees – Swarm
   Geese – Flock
   Lions – Pride
   Cows – Herd

2. Wolves – Pack
   Gorillas – Band
   Dolphins – Pod
   Puppies – Litter

3. Cow – Moo
   Horse – Neigh
   Wolf – Howl
   Cat – Meeow
   Duck – Quack
   Owl – Hoot
   Sheep – Bleat
   Lion – Roar
   Dog – Bark

## QUIZ 43: GUESS WHAT: FOOD

1. Rice
2. Spaghetti
3. Cheese
4. Watermelon
5. Lettuce
6. Peas
7. Coconut
8. Potato
9. Grapes
10. Ice cream
11. Chocolate
12. Ketchup
13. Pizza
14. Banana
15. Pumpkin

# ALL THE ANSWERS

## QUIZ 44: GUESS THE REST: WORDS
1. En garde
2. Eureka
3. Ahoy
4. Ciao
5. Onomatopoeic
6. Geology
7. Love
8. Dictionary
9. Punctuation
10. RSVP

## QUIZ 45: ODD ONE OUT: FOOD
1. What?: Beetroot
   Why?: A beetroot is a vegetable, all the others are fruits.

2. What?: Banana
   Why?: A banana is not a leafy vegetable, all the others are.

3. What?: Mushroom
   Why?: A mushroom is not a root vegetable, all the others are.

4. What?: Apple
   Why?: An apple is not a berry, all the others are.

5. What?: Fig
   Why?: A fig is not a nut, all the others are.

## QUIZ 46: QUIZ SHOW: ENVIRONMENT
1. b
2. a
3. c
4. c
5. b
6. c
7. a

## QUIZ 47: MISSING WORDS: SOUND
1. An echo
2. Tensions
3. Piano
4. Eardrum
5. Decibels
6. A vacuum
7. Sign language
8. Gets higher

## QUIZ 48: TRUE OR FALSE: WATER

| | | | |
|---|---|---|---|
| **1.** True | **5.** False | **9.** True | **13.** True |
| **2.** False | **6.** True | **10.** False | **14.** False |
| **3.** True | **7.** True | **11.** True | **15.** False |
| **4.** False | **8.** False | **12.** True | |

## QUIZ 49: OUT OF ORDER: GEOGRAPHY

**1.** Nile, Amazon, Mississippi, Congo, Niger, Seine

**2.** Pacific Ocean, Atlantic Ocean, Indian Ocean, Southern Ocean, Arctic Ocean

**3.** Mount Everest, K2, Kangchenjunga, Mount McKinley, Ben Nevis

## QUIZ 50: WORD JUMBLE: FOOD AND DRINK

| | | |
|---|---|---|
| **1.** Orange juice | **5.** Smoothie | **9.** Banana |
| **2.** Chow mein | **6.** Apple pie | **10.** Cheese |
| **3.** Cheese burger | **7.** Chocolate cake | |
| **4.** Ice cream | **8.** Spaghetti | |

## QUIZ 51: HALL OF FAME: ANIMALS

| | | | |
|---|---|---|---|
| **1.** b | **4.** b | **7.** b | **10.** b |
| **2.** a | **5.** c | **8.** a | |
| **3.** a | **6.** b | **9.** c | |

## QUIZ 52: MATCH UP: SPORTS

**1.**
Racket – Tennis
Baton – Relay
Bow and arrow – Archery
Shuttlecock – Badminton
Shin pads – Football
Club – Golf
Padded Gloves – Boxing
Poles – Skiing
Wickets – Cricket
Mat – Yoga

**2.**
Manchester United – England
Real Madrid – Spain
Juventus – Italy
Bayern Munich – Germany
Los Angeles Galaxy – USA
Fluminense – Brazil

## ALL THE ANSWERS

3.  Swimming – Pool          Ping pong – Table
    Football – Pitch          Baseball – Field
    Tennis – Court            Ice hockey – Rink
    Golf – Course             Bowling – Alley

## QUIZ 53: GUESS WHAT: SPORTS
1. Tennis        5. Basketball     9. Golf          13. Skiing
2. Football      6. Baseball      10. Ping pong     14. Swimming
3. Hockey        7. Fencing       11. Lacrosse      15. Archery
4. Cricket       8. Karate        12. Rowing

## QUIZ 54: GUESS THE REST: AROUND THE WORLD
1. Reptiles         5. Jaguar          9. Tectonic
2. Habitat          6. Tadpoles       10. Madagascar
3. Rainforest       7. Inland taipan
4. South America    8. Horse chestnut

## QUIZ 55: ODD ONE OUT: COUNTRIES
1.  What?: Greece
    Why?: Greece is in Europe, the other countries are in Asia.

2.  What?: Thailand
    Why?: Thailand is in Asia, the other countries are in Africa.

3.  What?: Peru
    Why?: Peru is in South America, the other countries are
    in Europe.

4.  What?: Norway
    Why?: Norway is in Europe, the other countries are in
    South America.

5.  What?: Australia
    Why?: Australia is in the Southern Hemisphere, all the
    other countries are in the Northern Hemisphere.

## QUIZ 56: HALL OF FAME: MUSIC

| | | | |
|---|---|---|---|
| 1. c | 4. c | 7. c | 10. a |
| 2. a | 5. b | 8. b | |
| 3. a | 6. a | 9. c | |

## QUIZ 57: GUESS THE REST: SPACE

| | | |
|---|---|---|
| 1. Saturn | 5. Astronomy | 9. Armstrong |
| 2. Ganymede | 6. Supernova | 10. Sputnik |
| 3. Hydrogen | 7. Gravity | |
| 4. Hubble | 8. Neptune | |

LEVEL THREE

## QUIZ 58: QUIZ SHOW: INVENTIONS

| | | | |
|---|---|---|---|
| 1. a | 3. b | 5. a | 7. a |
| 2. c | 4. c | 6. b | |

## QUIZ 59: MISSING WORDS: MATHS

| | |
|---|---|
| 1. Isosceles | 5. Shapes |
| 2. Acute | 6. Three dimensional |
| 3. 90 | 7. Circle |
| 4. Pentagon | 8. Percentage |

## QUIZ 60: TRUE OR FALSE: INVENTIONS

| | | | |
|---|---|---|---|
| 1. False | 5. False | 9. True | 13. False |
| 2. False | 6. True | 10. True | 14. False |
| 3. False | 7. False | 11. False | 15. True |
| 4. True | 8. False | 12. True | |

## QUIZ 61: OUT OF ORDER: COUNTRIES

1. Asia, Africa, North America, South America, Antarctica, Europe, Australia

## ALL THE ANSWERS

**2.** China, India, United States, Indonesia, Brazil, Pakistan, Nigeria

**3.** Greenland, Norway, Poland, Romania, Turkey, Egypt, Argentina

### QUIZ 62: WORD JUMBLE: COUNTRIES
**1.** Brazil
**2.** China
**3.** India
**4.** Iceland
**5.** Fiji
**6.** Hawaii
**7.** Russia
**8.** Germany
**9.** Antarctica
**10.** Reykjavik

### QUIZ 63: HALL OF FAME: SPACE
**1.** a
**2.** b
**3.** a
**4.** c
**5.** b
**6.** c
**7.** b
**8.** a
**9.** b
**10.** b

### QUIZ 64: MATCH UP: GEOGRAPHY
**1.**
England – London
Norway – Oslo
Thailand – Bangkok
China – Beijing
Egypt – Cairo
Argentina – Buenos Aires
Venezuela – Caracas
Vietnam – Hanoi
Jamaica – Kingstown
Spain – Madrid

**2.**
Rome – Europe
Tokyo – Asia
Chicago – North America
Caracas – South America
Sydney – Australia
Casablanca – Africa

**3.**
Belgium – Moules-frites
China – Peking duck
Germany – Bratwurst
Ireland – Colcannon
Pakistan – Biryani
Poland – Pierogi
Russia – Borscht
Spain – Paella
Turkey – Kebab

## QUIZ 65: GUESS WHAT: SPACE

1. Jupiter
2. Pluto
3. Saturn
4. The Sun
5. Earth
6. Comets
7. Asteroids
8. Black holes
9. The Moon
10. Stars
11. Atmosphere
12. Mars
13. Milky Way
14. Solar System
15. Galaxy

## QUIZ 66: GUESS THE REST: SEAS AND OCEANS

1. Amazon
2. Nile
3. South Africa
4. Pacific
5. Caspian Sea
6. Venice
7. New York
8. Persian Gulf
9. Arctic
10. Amstel

## QUIZ 67: ODD ONE OUT: SPORTS TEAMS

1. What?: All Blacks
   Why?: All Blacks is the New Zealand Rugby Union team, all the others are football teams.

2. What?: Chicago White Socks
   Why?: Chicago White Socks is a US baseball team, all the others are football teams.

3. What?: Manchester City
   Why?: Manchester City is a UK football team, all the others are US baseball teams.

4. What?: New Jersey Devils
   Why?: New Jersey Devils is a US ice hockey team, all the others are US baseball teams.

5. What?: Leeds Rhinos
   Why?: Leeds Rhinos is a UK Rugby League team, all the others are US ice hockey teams.

# ALL THE ANSWERS

## QUIZ 68: QUIZ SHOW: SPACE
1. c
2. b
3. a
4. a
5. b
6. a
7. c

## QUIZ 69: MISSING WORDS: SPACE
1. Saturn
2. Luna 2
3. Carbon dioxide
4. Mars and Jupiter
5. Astronomy
6. Dwarf planet
7. Jupiter
8. Mercury

## QUIZ 70: TRUE OR FALSE: MYTHS AND LEGENDS
1. True
2. True
3. False
4. False
5. True
6. False
7. False
8. True
9. False
10. False
11. True
12. True
13. True
14. True
15. True

## QUIZ 71: OUT OF ORDER: BIOLOGY
1. Femur (thighbone), Tibia (shinbone), Fibula (lower leg), Humerus (upper arm), Ulna (inner lower arm), Radius (outer lower arm)

2. Skin, Liver, Brain, Lungs, Heart

3. Sperm whale, Blue whale, Elephant, Dolphin, Human, Cat

## QUIZ 72: WORD JUMBLE: SCIENCE
1. Fossils
2. Hydrogen
3. Oxygen
4. Turbine
5. Kinetic
6. Fusion
7. Crater
8. Eye
9. Moon
10. Telescope

## QUIZ 73: HALL OF FAME: HISTORY
1. c
2. a
3. a
4. b
5. a
6. b
7. c
8. b
9. a
10. a

4. What?: Holly festival
   Why?: All the others are Chinese festivals, holly festival is not.

5. What?: Izanagi
   Why?: Izanagi is a Japanese diety, all the others are Hindu.

## QUIZ 78: OUT OF ORDER: GEOGRAPHY

1. California, Ohio, Tennessee, Kansas, Rhode Island, Vermont

2. Canada, Australia, United States, Italy, France, Finland

3. Russia, Australia, Egypt, Spain, Japan

## QUIZ 79: HALL OF FAME: WORLD KNOWLEDGE

| | | | |
|---|---|---|---|
| 1. c | 4. b | 7. b | 10. c |
| 2. a | 5. a | 8. a | |
| 3. c | 6. a | 9. a | |

## QUIZ 80: MATCH UP: HISTORY

1. Ming dynasty – China
   Renaissance – Italy
   Ottoman Empire – Turkey
   Mughal Empire – India
   Kamakura period – Japan
   Gilded Age – USA
   Victorian era – UK

2. Queen Elizabeth I –
      England
   Abraham Lincoln – USA
   Kaiser Wilhelm – Germany
   Emperor Qianlong – China
   Louis XVI – France
   King Constantine II –
      Greece
   Tony Abbott – Australia

3. Eiffel Tower – France
   Tower of Pisa – Italy
   Big Ben – England
   Taj Mahal – India
   The Great Sphinx – Egypt
   The Little Mermaid –
      Denmark
   Machu Picchu – Peru
   Brandenburg Gate –
      Germany
   Mount Rushmore – USA
   Saint Basil's Cathedral –
      Russia

## QUIZ 74: MATCH UP: MUSICAL INSTRUMENTS

**1.** Guitar – Frets
Cello – Scroll
Drum kit – Hi-hat
Flute – Lip plate
Trumpet – Bell
Piano – Key
Tambourine – Jingles
Xylophone – Bars
Accordion – Bellows

**2.** Flute – Woodwind
Cornet – Brass
Viola – Strings
Timpani – Percussion

**3.** Cello – Viola
Trombone – Tuba
Drums – Tambourine
Flute – Clarinet

## QUIZ 75: GUESS WHAT: COUNTRIES AND CITIES

**1.** Buenos Aires
**2.** Paris
**3.** Mecca
**4.** Sydney
**5.** Rome
**6.** La Paz
**7.** Venice
**8.** Dubai
**9.** Ireland
**10.** Vatican City
**11.** Germany
**12.** Italy
**13.** Chile
**14.** Hong Kong
**15.** Mumbai

## QUIZ 76: GUESS THE REST: MYTHOLOGY

**1.** Achilles
**2.** Troy
**3.** Minotaur
**4.** Olympus
**5.** Apollo
**6.** Celestial dragon
**7.** Medusa
**8.** Open sesame
**9.** Dwarves
**10.** Odysseus

## QUIZ 77: ODD ONE OUT: CULTURE

**1.** What?: Jujutsu
Why?: Jujutsu is a Japanese martial art, all the others are religions.

**2.** What?: Diwali
Why?: Diwali is a Hindu festival, all the others are Jewish celebrations.

**3.** What?: Castle
Why?: All the others are religious buildings, a castle is not.